Praise for S

"I am grateful that Sandy Boyd and Catherine Tran have taken the time and energy to write this book, *Spiritual Discovery: A Method for Discernment in Small Groups and Congregations*, to explain the prayer model in detail and to share how it has been taught and used in a variety of settings.. . . . As you read and practice and pray with the guidance of *Spiritual Discovery: A Method for Discernment in Small Groups and Congregations*, my prayer for you is that you will find deeper connections with the Spirit and with others. Use the material and stories in this wonderful book as a jumping off place. Feel free to experiment with it so it becomes yours. The prayer model is not a prescription to be followed to the letter. It is alive and expanding, so breathe more life into it, and see where the Spirit, which is the true teacher and director, guides you. You may be surprised!"

—from the Foreword by **Jane Vennard**, author of *A Praying Congregation*

"Adapted from Jane Vennard's practice of group prayer, Tran and Boyd give us the fruit of years of experience and provide careful attention to each aspect of this Spiritual Discernment Model. Those who are discernment guides will want to have this book."

—**Daniel Prechtel**, founder and spiritual director,
Lamb & Lion Spiritual Guidance Ministries

"The ancient practice of spiritual direction has caught the attention of many segments of the church in the last few decades, but congregations often struggle to identify how this practice can shape the ethos of their communities today. In this though-provoking, practical book, Tran and Boyd help congregations take a significant step toward integrating spiritual direction into their personal and communal discernment processes. Any pastor or lay person would benefit greatly from exploring and implementing the Prayer Model and Spiritual Discovery Method described in this book."

—**Angela Reed**, George W. Truett Theological Seminary

"Tran and Boyd have shared their experience and wisdom with us in this practical guide about the lifelong process of spiritual discovery and discernment. They have beautifully woven together the artistry of discovery and the skilled craft of discernment through the hospitality of storytelling, the gift of holy listening, and the power of silence."

—**Gil Stafford**, author of *When Leadership and Spiritual Direction Meet*

Spiritual Discovery

Spiritual Discovery

A Method for Discernment in Small Groups and Congregations

Catherine C. Tran and Sandra Hughes Boyd

An Alban Institute Book

ROWMAN & LITTLEFIELD
Lanham • Boulder • New York • London

Published by Rowman & Littlefield
A wholly owned subsidiary of The Rowman & Littlefield Publishing Group, Inc.
4501 Forbes Boulevard, Suite 200, Lanham, Maryland 20706
www.rowman.com

Unit A, Whitacre Mews, 26-34 Stannary Street, London SE11 4AB

British Library Cataloguing in Publication Information Available

Library of Congress Cataloging-in-Publication Data

Tran, Catherine C., 1959-
Spiritual discovery : a method for discernment in small groups and congregations / Catherine C. Tran
and Sandra Hughes Boyd.
pages cm
Includes bibliographical references.
ISBN 978-1-56699-773-7 (cloth : alk. paper) -- ISBN 978-1-56699-734-8 (pbk. : alk. paper) -- ISBN
978-1-56699-735-5 (electronic)
1. Prayer--Christianity--Study and teaching. 2. Discernment (Christian theology)--Study and teaching. 3. Small groups--Religious aspects--Christianity. I. Title.
BV214.T73 2015
253'.7--dc23
2014042268

Printed in the United States of America

To the Jane Vennard Supervision Group

and

the Working Group on Congregational Discernment of the Episcopal
Diocese of Colorado

Contents

Foreword

The ministry of spiritual direction is often symbolized by three chairs grouped together in a triangular pattern. One chair is for the director, the person whose main role is to listen, ask questions, and to lovingly respond. The second chair is for the one who has come to seek guidance, discuss an issue, tell a story, or to simply be in the presence of a listening heart. This person may be called the directee, the client, the seeker, or the story teller. The third chair remains empty, serving to remind both persons that the true director of the session, or the conversation, is the Spirit.

When teaching a course entitled Experiencing the Art of Spiritual Direction at the Iliff School of Theology in Denver, Colorado, I invited the students into pairs to practice speaking and listening to one another. I placed an empty chair beside them as that physical reminder of the holy presence while they practiced this one-on-one ministry of spiritual direction.

One week it occurred to me to fill that empty chair with a student observer, who was to watch and notice what was happening in the exchange. The students did not like the idea. They believed that the third person was there to evaluate and judge the others, and then to tell them after the session what they did wrong. I assured them that was not the purpose of the person in the third chair, but rather he or she was to be a witness to what was happening, to embody the Spirit's love and compassion for both director and directee. I also added that those in the third chair were not allowed to speak during or after the session—their presence was to be enough.

"Then what are we supposed to do?" they asked. "Pray," I responded, "in whatever way seems right to you. You might hold them in light, you could pray for your own heart to open to enable you to listen without judgment, or simply sit and breathe." I named the person in the third chair the compassionate observer.

With practice, the students discovered that the exchange was always enhanced by the presence of the compassionate observer. The directors reported that they felt supported and encouraged, that their questions and responses often seemed guided, and they were reminded they were doing holy work. The directees shared that they felt able to go more deeply into their stories and were able to share more honestly when they remembered the loving presence of God. By the end of the semester, they wondered how anyone could do spiritual direction without an actual compassionate observer being present!

When I moved on in that class from teaching one-on-one spiritual direction to teaching the process of group spiritual direction, it was a natural step to bring along the compassionate observers. I had learned group spiritual direction from Rose Mary Dougherty at the Shalem Institute in Washington, DC. In her model, one storyteller shares with three or four directors or responders. The guidelines were simple. A time for the process was decided upon by the group, usually thirty to forty-five minutes. The storyteller began the process by speaking without interruption. After some silence, a responder could ask a question or make an observation, prompting the storyteller to continue the story, look more deeply at the issue, or even take the story in a new direction. Other responders participated as they listened carefully and found within themselves questions that might facilitate the process. Periods of silence were to be included between questions and responses.

As I participated in this process of group spiritual direction, I found it challenging and exciting. As the storyteller, having more than one responder helped me view my issue from a variety of perspectives. As a responder, I liked sharing the responsibility for asking questions and offering possible insights with two or three others. The whole process felt rich and full of possibility.

When I introduced the model I had experienced on the Shalem retreat to my seminary students, I added the compassionate observers in the process. Surrounding the storyteller and responders in prayer continued the students' experience of the compassionate observer they had practiced in the triads. It also provided them the opportunity to be present and listen with no responsibility to speak.

As I watched the students practice, I noticed that they found it difficult to allow natural periods of silence during the process. Responders jumped in too quickly after the storyteller spoke. Questions followed with further questions coming rapidly, and the storyteller did not have enough time for reflection. I decided to add timed silent periods as a way to teach the students the benefit of including silence and stillness in group spiritual direction. This new model consisted of one storyteller, three or four responders, and at least two compassionate observers. I added a timekeeper to begin and end the periods of silence.

When Sandy Boyd called to ask if I would help begin an ecumenical peer supervision group for spiritual directors in the Denver metro area, this was the model I told her I would like to introduce. We gathered eight people and began the supervision process using what we came to call *the prayer model*. This group has lasted for over twenty years. Members have come and gone, and new people have been added. Over time we have refined the model, but the original spirit of the process has continued.

Catherine Tran was one of the early members, and it was she who took the prayer model to a judicatory group she was part of and started a program of teaching the model over a number of years. Other group members have taken the model into their teaching assignments, their congregations, and their spiritual formation groups. Adaptations are also being used in discernment groups, peer supervision groups, dream groups, and Bible studies. This prayer model seems now to have a life of its own.

I am grateful that Sandy Boyd and Catherine Tran have taken the time and energy to write this book, *Spiritual Discovery: A Method for Discernment in Small Groups and Congregations*, to explain the prayer model in detail and to share how it has been taught and used in a variety of settings. Releasing this prayer model into their hearts and hands for the benefit of others is a joy. Their willingness to continue to explore its many gifts and to encourage others to use it to promote prayerful discernment in a variety of settings warms my heart. I particularly appreciate their creativity in paying attention to how practicing the four roles in the model helps the participants deepen their prayer lives, the fruits of which they can then carry into the wider world.

As you read and practice and pray with the guidance of *Spiritual Discovery: A Method for Discernment in Small Groups and Congregations*, my prayer for you is that you will find deeper connections with the Spirit and with others. Use the material and stories in this wonderful book as a jumping off place. Feel free to experiment with it so it becomes yours. The prayer model is not a prescription to be followed to the letter. It is alive and expanding, so breathe more life into it, and see where the Spirit, which is the true teacher and director, guides you. You may be surprised!

Jane E. Vennard

Introduction

In the process of making a decision, a mindful person might gather data, list pros and cons, consult loved ones, or search the heart for answers. For those who understand themselves to be spiritual, this may also include reflection on how the sacred is part of the decision-making process. Such a spiritual person might turn for guidance and companionship to several sources: prayer, scriptures, a spiritual director, or the wisdom of a faith community. This is especially true when making significant, life-changing choices.

People considering ordination in the Episcopal Church in Colorado found that consultation with congregational groups appointed for that purpose was lacking an intentional spiritual dimension. Members of a congregational committee met with the person considering ordination and conducted what amounted to an employment interview, asking questions and applying whatever litmus tests they thought appropriate. The decision about ordination had taken on a secular institutional character which involved little or no opportunity for exploring the deeply spiritual nature of such a life-changing decision.

Church leadership turned to Catherine Tran for advice and recommendations about this situation. Under her leadership, the congregational discernment process was revised so as to include elements of prayer and spirituality. She incorporated Jane Vennard's prayer model, which provided the foundation for a method that congregational groups could use while meeting with persons seeking discernment about ordained ministry. In doing so, Catherine significantly reshaped the entire congregational discernment process. She was soon joined by Sandy Boyd, who assisted in development of the new discernment method and in training groups to use it. The materials for the congregational discernment process were updated and improved over the years in response to feedback and questions from these groups.

After some years training and observing what was happening in these congregational groups, we made a gratifying discovery. We watched the heart-felt engagement and transformation of participants as they practiced the discernment method. They were not only successful in assisting individuals in their discernment about ordained ministry. They also transferred the method into their own personal lives, developing practices of prayerful discernment which helped them make choices about education, careers, relationships, and faith-life participation. Some experienced a greater openness to unexpected or alternative outcomes for their decisions. Others celebrated new ways of listening, speaking, seeing, and participating in the world. Some learned how to be more compassionate as they observed themselves and others in the world. The use of the discernment method was a spiritually fulfilling experience for participants in a variety of contexts and at a number of levels.

People in the congregational groups also began to see how the discernment method could be used in ways that went far beyond the limited application to the Episcopal ordination process. Groups formed to help individuals practice spiritual discernment in making life-changing decisions. Other groups found that the method could be used for discernment in congregational committees and leadership councils. They felt empowered in new ways as they engaged in communal spiritual decision-making. These decisions now included an element of prayer that had been lacking and the results were surprising and delightful.

At the same time, we were aware of an interesting dynamic in church governance. Congregations are most often governed by groups that come together to make decisions on behalf of the whole body. Even those with a more authoritarian style of governance include groups that govern themselves and make their own decisions. It is quite customary for these groups to use a secular business model to guide their decision-making. A church governing council may open and close its meetings in prayer, but what happens in between can appear more like a business meeting with participants debating product choices than like a church council making spiritually enabled decisions. Somehow, the presence and voice of the Spirit is left out of the very decisions that should be spiritually grounded. Indeed, council leaders and members may be lacking the knowledge of how to become spiritually discerning in making communal decisions.

As we continued to observe the prayer model and discernment process functioning in church groups, we began to envision how a spiritual discernment method might be used by a variety of groups with a diversity of goals in a number of settings. We set to work formulating the spiritual discernment method for groups and individuals that is described in this book and named it the "Spiritual Discovery Method."

This is a practical, how-to book. Our goal is to offer here a method that any group can use to make decisions intentionally based on a spiritual foundation. The Spiritual Discovery Method equips a seeker, a lay leader, or a pastor with a description of the structure and skills needed to form a group and build it into an effective discerning group for community members. Other groups that might use the Spiritual Discovery Method include a book study group, a conflict management group, or a workplace task force. Throughout the book you will find stories of ways the skills learned in the practice of the Spiritual Discovery Method may be exercised "in the world." Practice of this method leads to growth in individual and collective spiritual wisdom that in turn leads to decision-making that is spiritually grounded.

We begin our account of the Spiritual Discovery Method in part 1 by providing a description and explanation of the Vennard Prayer Model, a process for guiding prayer in small groups, which serves as a foundation for other methods. Part 2 introduces, describes, and interprets the Spiritual Discovery Method, which expands upon the Vennard Prayer Model by adding space for group discussion and exploration. The method provides a structure for discernment in small groups and congregations. Part 3 takes an in-depth look at the compassionate observer—a seemingly straightforward, deceptively simple role in the Spiritual Discovery Method that proves both challenging and rewarding for many participants. Finally, Part 4 consists of stories and examples of how the Spiritual Discovery Method has been put to use in a variety of groups. These stories, as with the stories throughout the book, have been constructed as composites. By that we mean that they have been compiled from our own experience and from stories we have heard about how the Spiritual Discovery Method has been used. Except for our own names, the names and places have been changed for purposes of confidentiality. As you find it helpful, feel free to turn to the stories in part 4 for a sampling of the ways this method can be put to real-life use in a community.

We have been blessed to experience the power of spiritually focused discernment in a number of groups we have observed and learned about. Out of those observations and personal experiences, we share this transformative process with our readers. In this book, we have provided a method that groups can use to make spiritually grounded decisions and experience for themselves the power of spiritually focused discernment. We are confident that this method will be successful for your group. It is well-tested and has been proven over years of teaching, practice, application, and analysis. Both individuals and congregations can take heart in the openness and intention that are integrated into the process that we offer here. May you discover manifold blessings as you undertake this journey and find empowerment to make holy and fulfilling decisions for yourself, for your community, and for the world.

Catherine C. Tran and Sandra Hughes Boyd

I

The Prayer Model

From a young age, piano practice and recitals were a regular part of my (Catherine's) life. I enjoyed going into my practice room where I worked intently on technique and music making. I didn't enjoy the recitals as much. One thing I remember is feeling terribly exposed as I sat at the piano performing for audiences large and small. Everyone was looking at and listening to *me*! Everyone would hear my mistakes. That stage can be a lonely place. The soloist is responsible for every sound that comes out of the instrument for good or ill and receives all the accolades as well as criticism.

Well-rounded musicians balance this solo work with ensemble experiences. Practice sessions with groups focus on precise rhythm, blending with other instruments, tone, and various aspects of working together as a group. Musicians debate the musical interpretation and listen intently to each other as they play together. I enjoyed ensemble performances, but even more, I valued the group work and process of creativity. During those hours of practice together, I learned how musicians can begin to know each other so well that they can anticipate how their fellow musicians will play and what they are thinking at particular points in the music. The experience of working together to create beautiful music is gratifying and formative in ways that a solo performance is not, which for all its richness is a solitary experience.

Prayer is also a solitary experience at times. When I go into my prayer closet, my intention is to be alone with the Spirit. It is a time for deeply intimate reflection and conversation between me and the Spirit with nothing to disturb, distract, or interfere, except perhaps my own distracted thoughts. One of my spiritual discoveries in the prayer closet is that profound sense of what it means to be alone before God, simply standing as an individual in the presence of God without buffer or intermediary. God looks at and listens to *me*! The prayer closet can be a lonely place. It is a place to discover the self in relation to God, where each characteristic of the self is magnified by quiet solitude. It is a useful and necessary aspect of a spiritually examined life. And it is a terribly exposed experience—in a sense, a solo performance.

Prayer is not confined to the solitary experience in our prayer closets. A balanced prayer life includes ensemble experiences, such as congregations coming together for worship services and gathering for intercessory prayer, friends coming together to pray for each other, or the spiritually inquisitive joining a meditation group. As with musicians in ensembles, the experience of praying with others is different from a solo performance. Group prayer experiences expand our understanding of prayer, encourage us to observe a discipline, keep us from going off track, and provide accountability, among other things. Groups that pray together invite intimacy in relationships and provide members with a profound experience of spiritual companionship. An entirely new and different work of art emerges to complement the work that takes place in the solitude of the prayer closet. A well-rounded prayer life includes both solitary prayer experiences and group experiences.

Chapter One

Jane Vennard's Prayer Model

Jane Vennard's Prayer Model is an effective tool in any discernment process. It offers groups a structure for praying together that includes silence and listening and helps participants steep a process of discernment in prayer and spiritual attentiveness. It is a simple and orderly way for groups to gather in prayer. The Vennard Model draws us out of our individual prayer closets and, like musicians playing together in an ensemble, opens up a world of learning and wisdom that comes with a group experience.

Here in chapter 1, we will focus on the framework of the Vennard Model, which includes a description of the physical setting, participants' roles within the prayer, and the prayer order. The Vennard Model is the foundation of the Spiritual Discovery Method described in this book. In chapters 2 through 7, we will take a more in-depth look at the model, paying particular attention to the skills and disciplines that participants may discover and nurture as they practice the Prayer Model.

THE PHYSICAL SETTING OF THE PRAYER MODEL

The place where the group gathers for prayer needs to be large enough to accommodate the group sitting in one large circle and also flexible enough so that chairs can be moved into two concentric circles. It should be private and free from distractions such as noisy classrooms, telephones, or people inadvertently intruding.

As the group comes together, there should be several prayer tools on hand:

- A prayer chime, which is used to lead the group through the prayer process. A chime produces a gentle tone that marks periods of silence and speaking. One type of prayer chime is made with a metal bar (such as what you might see in a wind chime) wired to a small wooden block. Another type, a singing bowl, also known as a Tibetan singing bowl, consists of a brass bowl that sits on a small beanbag or cushion. Both chimes come with a wooden mallet.
- A watch with a second hand for the timekeeper.
- A candle and matches or a lighter.
- A printed order of the Prayer Model for the timekeeper to follow. Extra copies may be provided for participants, if desired.

Each participant should be provided with a comfortable, straight-backed chair. Initially, the chairs are arranged in two concentric circles, as shown in figure 1. There are four chairs in the inner circle for the seeker and responders and additional chairs in the outer circle for the timekeeper and compassionate observers.

PARTICIPANTS' ROLES IN THE PRAYER MODEL

The Prayer Model requires a minimum of eight participants: a seeker, three responders, a timekeeper, and three or more compassionate observers. A sufficient number of compassionate observers is required to adequately surround the inner circle. Without at least three compassionate observers, which hold the group in prayer, the group may begin to lose its focus and sense of safety.

The Seeker

The seeker sits in the inner circle. She comes to the prayer with a dilemma, a question, or a story. She may present a significant life transition or recurrent spiritual dilemma. The seeker's intention is to bring spiritual awareness to the situation or dilemma. She may, for example, hope to understand how the Spirit is speaking to her predicament or might be looking for options about which way to turn. Perhaps she shares something that she would like to cope with more effectively or a situation that she hopes to understand differently.

Sometimes a seeker may have a well-organized presentation with some hopes or goals in mind for what she would like to accomplish. At other times, the topic may be less defined and the seeker may come with an openness and

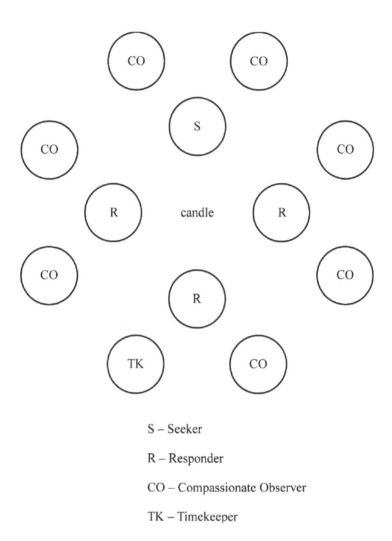

S – Seeker

R – Responder

CO – Compassionate Observer

TK – Timekeeper

Figure 1

willingness to follow the Spirit in prayer. However, if the seeker comes with the expectation that the dilemma will be miraculously resolved or the way ahead will be crystal clear, she will most likely be disappointed. The seeker should bring only an expectation that she will see the situation with new eyes, for example, or will be able to approach the dilemma more creatively.

The Responders

The responders take their places in the inner circle with an expectation that they will be listening to the seeker and offering brief comments in response. They also come with a willingness to hear to how the Spirit speaks to the seeker through them, and they offer these promptings as "gifts" to the seeker. These gifts may include observations of what they have seen and heard from the seeker or "mirroring," an image such as a mountain stream, a metaphor, a passage of scripture, or a thought-provoking question for the seeker's reflection. For example, a responder might offer an image from the 23rd Psalm. Or a responder may "mirror" the seeker by noting that each time the seeker mentioned a certain situation, she smiled.

The Compassionate Observers

The compassionate observers sit in the outer circle and do not speak during the prayer. They hold the process in prayer in order to create a sacred "container" for those in the inner circle. This container enfolds the inner circle and is a symbol of God's embracing presence. It helps the seeker and responders to feel safe and focused. The presence of the compassionate observers reminds participants that they are immersed in the Spirit. Compassionate observers are loving, non-judgmental witnesses of the work of the inner circle. Compassionate observers take on this role with the awareness that it also offers a unique and powerful opportunity for their own spiritual development.

The Timekeeper

The role of the timekeeper is to guide the group through the Prayer Model. The timekeeper keeps track of the time and the process while also serving as a compassionate observer. The timekeeper allows the others to pay full attention to their own participation in the prayer.

THE ORDER OF THE PRAYER MODEL

The seeker and responders take their places in the inner circle. The outer circle is composed of the compassionate observers and the timekeeper. The seeker and the timekeeper should sit so they can maintain eye contact with each other. The timekeeper takes charge of the prayer chime and watch. She may remind participants to turn off their cell phones. The lighted candle is placed in the center of the circles, either on the floor or on a small, low table.

After all are seated and quiet, the process begins with a brief prayer or sentence offered by the timekeeper. This is followed by a strike of the chime, which signals the beginning of three minutes of silence. Another strike of the chime closes the period of silence, and the seeker takes up to ten minutes to share a question or dilemma. If the seeker takes less than ten minutes, the timekeeper does not wait for the full ten minutes to pass before striking the chime but rings it to begin the silence as soon as the seeker has finished. It may be necessary for the timekeeper to give the seeker a signal that the ten minutes are about to end, so the seeker can bring the sharing to a close. If the seeker is still speaking at the end of ten minutes, the timekeeper rings the chime, and the seeker stops speaking.

Another period of three minutes of silence begins. At the close of the silence, the chime marks the beginning of the time during which the responders speak. Each briefly responds once, allowing a few moments between responses. There is no chime between the responders, and the seeker does not reply to each response. After all the responders have spoken, the timekeeper strikes the chime to begin another three minutes of silence. The chime again closes the silence, and the seeker takes a couple of minutes to describe insights, share learnings, or reflect on what has been heard from the responders. The seeker may also choose to say nothing more and simply thank the responders. This is followed by a one-minute period of silence, at the end of which the timekeeper strikes the chime and closes the prayer by saying, "Amen."

The prayer takes about thirty minutes, less if participants don't use the full amount of time allotted for each speaking step. The process is outlined as follows, the chime being indicated by the asterisk:

*Brief opening prayer
*Three minutes of silence
*Up to ten minutes for the seeker to present
*Three minutes of silence
*Each responder speaks briefly
*Three minutes of silence
*Seeker takes up to three minutes to share closing thoughts
*One minute of silence
*"Amen"

It is helpful for the timekeeper to quietly note each step as the process moves along. For example, she may say, "The seeker has up to ten minutes to share" or "Three minutes of silence." It is also important for the timekeeper to gently provide a word or two of guidance if a participant speaks out of turn. The verbal guidance of the timekeeper is useful for all of the participants, freeing them from concern about the details of the process itself and thus enabling them to fully enter into the rhythm of the prayer.

Participants then rearrange their chairs into one large circle and take a few minutes to review or debrief the process. It is not appropriate to talk about what someone said, make further comments that they think might be useful to the seeker, or express an opinion about what the responders said. Only the process itself may be discussed. Content is being discussed if, for example, a participant begins a sentence, "When the seeker said . . . " or "If I was a responder, I would have said . . . " It is appropriate, however, for participants to mention a distraction in the room, personal feelings evoked by the process, concern about the length of the silence, or other experiences of the process. The Spiritual Discovery Method, not the Prayer Model, does include some topical discussion. Later, we will examine how topical discussion beyond the debriefing fits into the Spiritual Discovery Method as a whole.

The purpose of debriefing is to improve how the group is conducting the process, to respond to any changes that need to be made in order to follow the process more closely, or to gain a deeper understanding of the model's structure. The debriefing is important because it helps the group grow in its understanding of the process and become more competent in its practice of the Prayer Model. Even for groups that have experienced the model for years, the debriefing is beneficial.

THE PRAYER MODEL AT WORK FOR INDIVIDUAL DISCERNMENT

Philip was in his early thirties and had spent the last several years teaching chemistry at the local high school. For several months he had been dissatisfied with his work. Although he enjoyed being with students, he was bored with teaching and frustrated by the politics of the school system. He was thinking about going back to school to get a doctorate in chemistry and eventually working in a research lab. But Philip wondered if he was up to going back to school and thought he would miss his interactions with students. He couldn't decide what to do.

A good friend at church told Philip about a group in their congregation that was available to help church members discern about how the Spirit might be speaking in their lives. He said that they might be able to help Philip decide about leaving his job and going back to school. Since Philip had been wondering how his faith might inform his decision, he was intrigued by the idea of praying with others about his career and inviting the Spirit into his decision. He did some research into what the group offered and decided to ask the group leader if he might bring his dilemma before them. He was invited to attend their next meeting.

The evening of the meeting, Philip was a bit nervous about discussing his situation with the discernment group. He had been asked to prepare a short presentation summarizing his predicament and sharing his questions about it. He knew some of the group members, but others he had not met. It seemed strange to share his thoughts and feelings with people whom he did not know well, but the group welcomed him warmly and made him comfortable. After some introductions, the group leader described the Prayer Model. She said that they would pray first and then, after a short break, spend some time exploring Philip's dilemma. She explained that the Prayer Model followed by some discussion of the situation were the two main components of the Spiritual Discovery Method they used. Philip relaxed a bit as they entered into prayer.

By the end of the evening, Philip was amazed about how the Spirit had spoken to him through the discernment group. He was deeply moved by the power of the prayer, and he felt like he could trust the group. They had given him some new ways to think about his situation. He felt empowered and was excited to continue to explore his career options. He was glad that his decisions about his future could be spiritually grounded in prayer and looked forward to meeting with the group a few more times over the next months.

At those meetings with the discernment group, Philip prayerfully offered his confusion and questions. He was so grateful for the insights that came with each session. The group helped Philip reflect on his own strengths and weaknesses, the desires of his heart, his practical situation, how his career move might affect others, and many other aspects of his decision. With each meeting, Philip grew in self-awareness and reflected deeply about how the Spirit was present in his life. Discernment about life-changing decisions no longer seemed as mysterious as it had.

Over the months, Philip began to realize that teaching was what he truly loved to do. He decided to remain in his job and felt at peace with his decision, believing that teaching was the Spirit's deepest desire for him. He recognized that he was a gifted teacher and how much the interaction with students meant to him. He also began to see clearly how he might change his own behavior to address his boredom. He even thought of ways he could change his interactions with the administration and school board to help not only himself, but other teachers as well. With this new energy and enthusiasm for his work, Philip began to enjoy teaching again. Even his students noticed a difference in him.

At Philip's last meeting with the discernment group, he expressed his gratitude for the way they had listened to him and helped him see how the Spirit was present in his life. They, in turn, shared how his dilemma had helped each of them to reflect on their own vocations and how refreshing it was for them to examine those choices with new eyes. Philip thought that if he ever needed some spiritual counsel or was looking for someone to talk to about spiritual things, he would use a group discernment process like this again.

The Prayer Model is a structured way to bring groups together for contemplative prayer and discernment. Its simplicity makes it accessible and useful in a variety of situations, such as vocational discernment, study groups, or congregational decision-making. The group supports the individual who seeks to bring the presence of the Spirit into a situation through silence, listening, and reflection. Seekers who come with open hearts and minds to groups that practice the model will discover a powerful resource for decision-making. The Prayer Model has proven itself to be an effective tool for those who are making decisions.

In addition, prayer following this model transforms group life and helps individuals to grow and change. It is a rich ensemble experience. We have often seen how effectively the Prayer Model can build trust in groups and help individuals shift out of stuck places. As group members become more proficient in listening to the Spirit and to others, they grow in wisdom and self-awareness. Members of groups discover that they can be instruments of the Spirit and become companions for each other as they navigate the spiritual experience. Transformation happens!

Chapter Two

The Prayer Model in Depth

St. John's Church was beginning the process of recruiting new members for their leadership council. They wanted to encourage a spiritual approach to congregational leadership by starting with a communal process by which prospective members could prayerfully consider their call to serve on the council. The congregation's pastor was familiar with the Spiritual Discovery Method because one of the church's staff members trained groups that were learning to use the Vennard Prayer Model. He asked her to work with him in leading the potential new council members through a prayerful discernment process.

The prospective members were provided with information about council membership responsibilities and asked to pray about their call to serve as they prepared to pray and discern with the council. Each potential member was invited to take the seeker's chair and tell the group why they felt they were being called to membership on the council. They were asked to describe the gifts they might bring to the council and how they saw themselves contributing to the council's ministry of leadership.

After meeting with the council and using the Prayer Model, each of the prospective members left with a much clearer understanding of what it would mean to serve on the council and how they might be called to serve the church. One woman had come to the meeting somewhat reluctant to join the council but had changed her mind after praying with the group. Another prospective member saw that his call was to continue his ministry managing the church's buildings and grounds instead of joining the council. He said he had gained new energy for his present ministry from his experience with the Prayer Model.

A third potential member had served on the council previously and had felt then that its deliberations were overly business-like and even at times uncomfortably contentious. He was reluctant to rejoin the council, but after praying with the group, he realized that though the council would face challenging decisions, they would be made in an environment of communal prayer. He agreed to serve again.

Another potential member who was also an "old hand" at council leadership declined to participate as the seeker in the Prayer Model. He did allow himself to be persuaded to attend the meeting even though he thought it would be a waste of time. He was impressed with how the Prayer Model helped others with their discernment. When he saw that others were neither judged nor advised about their decisions, he was eager to try the seeker's role and did so. All five prospective members took part as seekers in the prayer. Four joined the council with a clear sense of being called and an appreciation that their gifts for ministry would be appreciated. The fifth recognized that his gifts were also needed in the congregation but could most fruitfully be put to use in other ways. The discernment exercise had helped the group prayerfully decide the membership of the new council. They also saw how the Prayer Model could be a useful tool in future deliberations.

As the new council convened for its first meeting, it faced a major challenge in the growing recognition that a capital campaign was needed in order to provide much needed improvements to the church's programs and facilities. The previous council had been unable to move ahead with this project, arguing that economic conditions were poor and that it had been only a few short years since the completion of a major building project. Though council members acknowledged that failing to take on a capital campaign had significantly restricted the church's ministries, they feared that a new campaign would be doomed from the start.

As the new council gathered and began to discuss—again—the pros and cons of a new capital campaign, they had an entirely new experience of this previously contentious matter. They said they felt more open to possibilities and risk-taking. One continuing council member realized that he had been acting out of fear rather than faith. Another member reported a new understanding of her responsibilities as a spiritual leader. She needed to let go of her anxiety about the campaign and join the others in stepping out in faith. And so they initiated a new capital campaign.

The council members reported that all of them had grown in their appreciation of the spiritual dimension of their leadership. Even the process of coming to this major decision had been less quarrelsome and had in fact been more prayerful and thoughtful. They were able to listen more deeply to each other. Their relationships were stronger and communication was more respectful. Since they had agreed to serve out of a sense of call and not out of a sense of duty, their commitment to the congregation had been strengthened. The Spirit had been intentionally invited into their midst, and the nature of the council's decision-making and even its entire communal life had been fundamentally transformed by their prayerful discernment.

PRAYER MODEL FUNDAMENTALS

It is important for individual participants to prepare their hearts and minds for prayer and discernment. There are attitudes and practices that, once developed, will strengthen the practice of the prayer. Participants will discover the importance of being open to the guidance of the Spirit and trusting and practicing the process as it is outlined here. They must be committed to the group discipline and practice and, over time, will find that the Spiritual Discovery Method is learned best by doing it. Experience is the best teacher.

There are several fundamentals that we have learned are most beneficial to the success of the Prayer Model. They are observing the prayer order, learning by experience, developing discipline, practicing silence, creating sacred space, growing in self-awareness, opening the heart and mind, and trusting the process. Those who have come to the prayer grounded in these fundamentals have gotten the most out of the practice. We urge participants to pay attention to these fundamentals as they learn the Prayer Model and Discernment Method. With continued practice, participants can learn and grow in each of the fundamentals, and with that growth, the prayer becomes more effective.

OBSERVING THE PRAYER ORDER

As a group becomes more proficient in practicing the Prayer Model, members begin to discover how the structure and rhythm of the speaking, listening, and silence creates a spiritual container that promotes openness to each other, to self, and to the Spirit. Engaging in one focused activity at a time, such as listening or speaking, frees participants to be fully present to what is happening in the moment.

The seeker is free to let go of those things that he may have neglected to say and trust that what was said was sufficient. Because the prayer order prohibits any questions to clarify what the seeker has said, the responder is obliged to surrender any curiosity about what was *not* said, focusing instead on what *was* said. The compassionate observer is free to let go of anything that she thinks ought to be said. Letting go of what any participant thinks should have been said requires that all participants trust the Spirit to make available as appropriate—and no doubt at some other time and place—any contributions that *might have been* offered.

Put another way, everyone is free to let go of expectations. What is in the moment simply is, and participants are encouraged to trust it. The prayer order, carefully observed, provides a trustworthy framework within which participants can experiment with the freedom of being in the moment and taking what comes without hesitation.

LEARNING BY EXPERIENCE

The Prayer Model is best learned through experience. It is easy to learn and requires no special skills or knowledge, which allows for groups to practice it effectively from the beginning. Participants learn how to do the prayer, experience the prayer, and then examine the experience in the debriefing. The learnings from the debriefing are applied in the next prayer experience. This in turn is examined and serves to inform the next experience. It doesn't take long for participants to become proficient at the prayer. Gathering on a regular basis to practice the prayer is essential so that participants can become comfortable with the order and can then focus on what happens within the prayer rather than the prayer structure itself.

Although the structure of the prayer is consistent, the experience of it is never the same. This is true for participants in all roles. Each presentation by a seeker leads to a unique spiritual exploration. A compassionate observer may find a seeker's presentation confusing and troubling but, during the next few weeks, reflect on her experience and come to realize that she has some similar spiritual questions and proceed to explore them for herself. The next time the group gathers for prayer, the same compassionate observer finds another seeker's presentation uplifting and inspiring. As she further reflects during the following weeks, she is grateful for the joy in her life. The two experiences were entirely different even though the prayer structure was unchanged.

DEVELOPING DISCIPLINE

A discipline is an activity that one regularly undertakes for the purpose of accomplishing a goal, developing a skill or talent, or improving one's character. People who seem to be more disciplined have usually worked at becoming that way. They see the results of their discipline and value the results. The discipline is worthwhile. The first step in developing a discipline is to create a supportive environment. Next, make a commitment to the discipline and keep it. At the beginning and perhaps for some period of time, the commitment must often be renewed. Eventually, the discipline becomes a part of one's regular way of life.

For both individuals and groups, prayer is a discipline. A well-rounded prayer discipline includes a private component, such as meditation or praying for others, and a communal component, such as weekly worship or a regular prayer group. Participation in a group prayer discipline provides accountability to one's peers. Group members count on one another to be present and engaged. The Vennard Prayer Model is a communal prayer discipline that can be of significant benefit to any individual, group, or community that practices it regularly. It can also be transformative for the community of which the group is a part. The leadership council at St. John's Church, for example, came to the Prayer Model aiming to address individual as well as corporate goals. They wanted to discern each participant's call to serve on the council as well as a corporate hope for strengthening the council's spiritual leadership. Both goals were met.

PRACTICING SILENCE

Silence is a prominent feature of the Prayer Model. Some participants may be new to the experience of silence in groups, and others, depending on their own particular history with silence, may enter into it with varying degrees of comfort. If one's personal experience is negative, such as being silenced as punishment, it is important for this person to be aware of that when encountering the group silence in the Prayer Model.

Silence in the prayer serves a number of purposes, most importantly enabling focused listening to the self, the speaker, and the Spirit. For the seeker, the silence provides a brief respite following the presentation. Later in the prayer, it is an opportunity for the seeker to reflect about what she hears from the responders.

For responders, it provides an opportunity for focused listening. Because there will be a period of silence during which responders can formulate a response, they are freed to listen attentively when the seeker and others speak. During the silence, the responders can attend to what the Spirit is offering, filtering out their own "agendas" (and perhaps noting them for future reflection). It is an opportunity for responders to notice how well they trust that whatever they offer will be helpful—by way of the Spirit—despite having no control over the gift the Spirit offers.

For the compassionate observers—and indeed, all participants—the silence is a time to still the heart and mind so that the Spirit can be heard. This inner quiet is for both those who are giving voice to their thoughts and for those who do not speak. It is also an opportunity for participants to listen to the Spirit and receive inspiration for their own spiritual exploration. In the lives of those who continue to practice it, silence becomes more fruitful as they spend more time listening to the Spirit.

CREATING SACRED SPACE

A place that is set aside for holy use is sacred space. The time, place, people, words, thoughts, and prayers within that space are all set apart from the everyday. As they enter into prayer, participants are superbly aware of the presence of the Spirit within the circle. Participants who are responsible for selecting or setting up the place where the group will gather may want to be mindful of the sacred use of the space, as hospitality to the Spirit is reflected in how the place is prepared and maintained.

In the Prayer Model, the compassionate observers in the outer circle mark the border of the sacred space or container. Within the container, what happens is understood as holy and treated with the respect and awe that holiness inspires. The communal prayer of the group invites the Spirit into the space. Participants are mindful of the personal responsibility of each one to help maintain the integrity of the space by filling it with listening prayer.

GROWING IN SELF-AWARENESS

The self-aware participant will be attentive to his own needs. For example, if he cannot hear the other speakers, he may first address this by moving closer where he can see their faces. If that doesn't work, he may ask the speakers to speak up. In such a case, self-awareness is not only helpful to the individual who is self-aware but may also be helpful to others in the group. If a participant needs to leave the group early for some unavoidable reason, before the session begins she tells the group when she will be leaving and apologizes for the disruption, which she then tries to keep at a minimum.

Being aware of what is going on within oneself spiritually, physically, emotionally, and intellectually is important. For example, a person may feel fidgety or notice butterflies in the stomach during the group silence. This is an opportunity for him to reflect on what it is about group silence that causes discomfort and work on changing his response to it. In this way, self-awareness helps a participant minimize internal distractions and participate in the prayer in the most beneficial way.

A self-aware person will also keep healthy boundaries around her own struggles, identifying any tendency to blame, project, or become entangled in others' issues. For example, if one is annoyed by what someone has said, she can look within to see what has triggered the irritation and acknowledge that it is her issue and not the speaker's. Once she has "owned' her annoyance, she can choose to change it.

OPENING THE HEART AND MIND

When participants come to the prayer to discern a direction or make a decision, they sometimes hold on to a preconceived outcome. In order to practice genuine discernment, it is essential to hold these preferences lightly and to open the heart and mind to the subtle movement of the Spirit. Participants must be receptive to conversion of their preferences. They must also be open to many possible outcomes of their discernment. It is only with this state of heart and mind that authentic listening can take place and seekers can hear the collective wisdom of the Spirit-led group. With open hearts and minds, seekers can perceive the movement of the Spirit and take in new thoughts and ideas. This openness encourages creative thinking and welcomes the surprises that can surface during prayerful discernment.

Individuals or groups typically have a preferred outcome in mind. A seeker may come with answers that are already determined and have an expectation that the predetermined decision will be confirmed or "blessed" by the Spirit. When this happens, listening stops and creative thinking shuts down. There is no room for discernment to take place. It is important to come to the prayer with an awareness of these preferences and a willingness to have them challenged. Genuine discernment requires seekers hold lightly to strong preferences and begin to see and value other options.

TRUSTING THE PROCESS

Time and experience enable participants to trust the prayer process. As they learn to enter into it without reservation, the gifts of the prayer reveal themselves again and again. The Vennard Prayer Model is simple, allowing participants to focus on the Spirit rather than complicated prayer techniques such as breathing a certain way or maintaining particular postures. The predictable, repetitive nature of the Prayer Model creates a reliable framework within which participants can invite the Spirit of God to speak. If group members find themselves tempted to take short cuts or deviate from the prayer order, we encourage them to stay within the given structure. Elements of the process that don't seem to make sense at first—such as time limits or rules for speaking—eventually prove themselves to be useful even to the most impatient or skeptical. Because the prayer is learned primarily through practice, it takes time to understand the unfolding power and depth of the discipline. The prayer order creates a predictable, reliable structure that the participants come to trust. They can be more focused and attentive to the present moment rather than wondering what comes next. Maintaining the prayer order increases its effectiveness and allows participants to go deeper into the experience. The only surprises in the prayer are those presented by the Spirit!

Chapter Three

Hospitality

Prayer itself is an act of hospitality. At its most profound, it is about hospitality to the Spirit—consciously inviting the Spirit to be present in a particular moment. We practice interior hospitality when we invite the Spirit to speak to us in prayer and create a welcoming place into which the Spirit may speak. An invitation to speak implies an attitude of listening. We prepare a quiet place within—a place of waiting and listening—where the Spirit's voice is not drowned out by the clutter of busy thoughts. This is a place of emptiness that is waiting to be filled by the Spirit; a sanctuary of the soul. Hospitality to the Spirit is the foundation of our practice of hospitality to others and is reflected in the quality of that hospitality. It is something we practice in our hearts and souls and then reflect outwardly as we extend hospitality to others.

The Prayer Model, as the foundational component of the Spiritual Discovery Method, calls for careful attention to hospitality. Attention to preparation and details is important in order to be most hospitable, as the physical space reflects the inward practice. The Prayer Model provides an opportunity to extend hospitality to those who come to pray and discern together. Important elements of this hospitality include the preparation of the meeting place and gathering the tools. Attention to the setting and tools reflects care and commitment to the prayer. It helps the guests understand that their presence is desired and they are welcome. Hospitality is about both opening one's heart to the other and providing a pleasant physical space where people feel comfortable. It is about welcoming each other and welcoming the Spirit of God.

PREPARE A PLACE

The environment shapes the quality of the prayer experience. An attractive and well-equipped room can enhance any prayer practice, and it is important to create a space in which participants will feel welcome and at ease. The aesthetics of the room influence the experience of its occupants. Clutter, for example, can reflect disorganization and be distracting. Bad lighting affects mood. An oversized room diminishes the feeling of intimacy for the group. Attention to such details will make a difference in how participants experience the prayer.

The room needs to be large enough to accommodate a circle of chairs with an open space in the center. Tables need to be moved out of the way. We recommend padded chairs with straight backs that are easy to move. Furniture like that generally found in living rooms, such as sofas or armchairs, is not recommended because it is difficult to arrange in circles. Also, participants might be tempted to nap rather than pray!

When deciding on a gathering place, spend some time in the room and notice potential distractions. Listen for street noise, tend to the phone that needs to be turned off, feel the temperature, be aware of the lighting. Imagine the space on the day of the week and the time of the day when you will gather. Make sure the group will not be disturbed by other groups in the building.

As a group comes together to practice the Prayer Model, individual members will have different needs that should be addressed. If a participant is distracted by the lighting in the room, the group can decide to change the lighting level or type (if possible). If another is particularly sensitive to outside noise, do what you can to minimize it. It is also important to accommodate group members' physical disabilities. If a participant has difficulty hearing, he should sit in a place where he can hear. Being sensitive to the needs of the group by paying attention to the quality of the space will improve the experience for everyone.

Finally, it is crucial to pay attention to the group's need for privacy. If the space is one that someone might walk through unexpectedly, such as a sanctuary or larger hall, you may wish to relocate your group or make signs requesting privacy. Make sure that your prayer exchanges will not be overheard by someone occupying a nook around a corner. Do what is possible to ensure that confidentiality is protected.

GATHER THE TOOLS

The quality of the prayer experience will be affected by the characteristics of the tools you use. They may become a distraction if they are intended for a different purpose or not conducive to prayerful reflection and silence.

One of the most important tools is the prayer chime or singing bowl. Both of these have a resonant tone and are available in different pitches: the smaller the chime or bowl, the higher the pitch. Both chimes and bowls are inexpensive and easy to find. Other types of bells may detract from the prayer experience, so substitutions are discouraged. Once, we worked with a group that chose to use a cow bell while they waited for the prayer chime they had ordered to arrive. All agreed that the bell was so strongly associated with grazing cows that they found it distracting. Before leading the prayer, it is helpful for the timekeeper to practice ringing the chime to produce a gentle sound.

The timekeeper needs to have a watch with a second hand. Any other type of timing device such as an hourglass, a timer, or a wall clock cannot be controlled or may make distracting noises. One group experimented with a three-minute egg timer. During the prayer, group members found themselves staring at the egg timer. This was mentioned during the debriefing, and everyone agreed that the timer had become a distraction. They elected to have the timekeeper return to using a watch.

A printed outline of the prayer order is a helpful guide for group members and is necessary for the timekeeper. Participants may depend on this guide as they learn the prayer order but gradually will come to depend on the time-keeper to provide the needed reminders at the appropriate places. When new members join a group, an outline should be available for their reference. Even those who consider themselves "old hands" at the Prayer Model contin-ue to find the printed outline helpful.

Because scents may be distracting or problematic for some, the candle should be unscented. It should be stable and placed on either a low table or the floor in a way that ensures it will not tip over or inadvertently be kicked. Be sure that it will burn for at least thirty minutes and that drips will be contained. Don't forget to bring matches or a lighter.

Learning to follow a spiritual discipline is supported by creating an envi-ronment that is hospitable to the discipline. As a skill—or an art—hospitality improves with practice. Setting aside the time, creating the place, and provid-ing appropriate tools are all things that can be done to nurture the practice of the group discipline. Setting aside time and careful preparation of place and tools are also important for the support of individual spiritual disciplines. Such an attitude of hospitality can change not only the way we pray, but the way we approach life. In addition to creating a physically pleasing space, practicing hospitality of the heart, mind, and spirit encourages openness and welcomes people, ideas, words, and inspiration.

Chapter Four

Participants' Roles in the Prayer Model

The space is prepared, and the group is gathered. It is time for everyone to choose how they will participate in the Prayer Model. Each of the four roles of seeker, responder, compassionate observer, and timekeeper is not only necessary for the group process but also teaches spiritual disciplines and provides a chance to practice them. As we explore the roles in the model, we will show how each contributes to the effective practice of the model and address some of the many possibilities for learning and practice that each role offers.

One of the gifts of the Prayer Model is that, with every session, group members are invited to practice the particular roles with their entire being. When a participant is the seeker, for example, he enters into that role with body, mind, and spirit. Participants practice the art of seeking, responding, observing, and serving (as timekeeper) by sitting in a particular place and focusing the spirit, mind, and body on a particular act. The whole self is invested in seeking, for example: searching with the intellect, exploring spiritually, and even physically occupying the seat of the seeker. By training the whole of the self to be a seeker, responder, compassionate observer, or timekeeper, the participant learns skills that are useful in a variety of life situations.

Each participant comes to the Prayer Model with unique experiences, gifts and weaknesses, and a certain level of willingness to risk. Some are more adventurous than others. Members of the group arrive with their own distinct degree of self-awareness. Some are more curious than others. Each person discovers something that will be unique to that individual. What we offer here are some of the discoveries that some of the participants have made as they have engaged in the Prayer Model. Participants who come to the model with openness to unlimited possibilities for learning and a desire to wrestle with spiritual questions will find that each new discovery opens the door to another.

THE SEEKER

One time, I (Sandy) was a seeker during the prayer. I was having difficulty articulating the dilemma I wanted to describe. My story circled around, bounced back and forth, and took off on tangents. I realized as I spoke that the responders and compassionate observers were probably as confused as I was about what I was trying to say. At the end of my sharing, I confessed how confused I was and apologized to my responders for being so scattered in my presentation.

The responders' offerings surprised me. They affirmed that my confusion had in fact been useful because it had enabled me to question my own story. And they noted that in the process of presenting my dilemma and naming my confusion, I could be more receptive to new ways of thinking. Although they admitted that their responses probably did not clarify my situation, they offered the hope that my taking the opportunity to "live into" my confusion would create an opening for the illumination I was seeking.

Confusion may be uncomfortable for a time, but it can provide a useful perspective. It is one manifestation of openness. It demonstrates a willingness and perhaps even an intense desire to solve a problem or find a direction. It can prompt creative thinking and earnest listening. Our confusion may move us into a place of holy indifference or detachment about *which* direction we take because our deeper desire may be just to *have* a direction. Any direction to take is better than none. Confusion creates the opportunity for us to detach from the outcome of our discernment and accept the guidance of the Spirit.

We all experience confusion from time to time, and when we do, having a group of companions with whom to sit and pray can be a great gift. Again and again as we come together in prayer, we make the refreshing discovery that we are not alone. Our companions have experienced similar questions and dilemmas about life, and thus the seeker presents a dilemma not only for herself but for others in the circle as well. It is not unusual to seek purpose in life, wonder about which way to turn, struggle with how to love best, feel challenged by difficult relationships, and wrestle with our shortcomings. The seeker's story is a gift in the midst of those dilemmas. Sharing one's questions and confusion with others takes a certain amount of humility, but that humility binds companions together as they ask the same questions and wrestle with the same challenges. As seekers, we talk about our questions and dilemmas and explore together. The companionship of others helps to shape a seeker's spiritual exploration.

The role of the seeker can be one of vulnerability. Opening a window into our own spiritual wonderings can be deeply self-revealing. We entrust our deepest questions, wounds, or dilemmas to the care of the group, as responders and compassionate observers listen with focus and intensity. The seeker experiences what it means and how it feels to be heard with such intense focus. When we discover ourselves wrapped in the care and respect that the circle of pray-ers offers, that willingness to be vulnerable becomes an opportunity for growth and healing. Vulnerability makes us stronger. In the prayer, we begin to learn the wisdom of vulnerability, when and with whom to practice it, and how it is an essential aspect of our spiritual growth.

The Prayer Model encourages us to pay attention to the act of seeking. When a seeker is reflecting ahead of time on what to present to the group, he organizes his thoughts and formulates his questions. He prepares to articulate complex ideas. His seeking becomes less haphazard and includes reflection and awareness that is invited by the prayer. The act of presenting requires that the seeker explain his dilemma to the group. Articulating confusion and vulnerability moves us to examine our thoughts and emotions. The act of seeking itself takes shape and becomes more focused and purposeful.

Bill wrote about his experience of becoming a seeker during his discernment process for ordained ministry. He said that at first he had been very uncomfortable in his role as seeker because he was very aware that it meant he had to be fully vulnerable with a group of people he knew but had never been with before on such a personal level.

He said that in the beginning he had no idea what to bring to the Prayer Model as a seeker and started that first session by sharing that with the group. This eased the tension for everybody, and Bill discovered that over time, serving as seeker became easier for him. He was able to identify, with the group, a number of issues, including some which kept him from being fully open during other aspects of his ordination discernment process. Some of them were issues with his family and neighbors, but he found that the majority of the issues concerned himself, his history and past, as well as where he was headed in the future.

After about a year, Bill reported that he came to cherish his role as seeker because he felt he was being protected by "an invisible force of love and compassion" made up of the responders and compassionate observers. He said that, amazingly, this force of love and compassion "channeled his prayers directly to God." Though some time had passed since this experience as a seeker, he concluded, "I still remember the lessons received from the responders during my time as a seeker."

The Seeker in the World

Group members have occupied the chair of the seeker and participated with all of the body, mind, and spirit, with intention and awareness, and they can take that same awareness and intention into other times of seeking. The Prayer Model brings the act of seeking to our attention, and that attention changes the nature of the search itself. Seekers become more aware of the practice of seeking and can make conscious choices about how they seek. The skill of seeking practiced in the world offers many gifts in return.

Seeking is a creative way of being as we look for solutions to the puzzles of life and examine dilemmas from various angles. A lifelong seeker is always open to new discoveries. We can open ourselves to unimagined possibilities rather than assuming we have all the answers and have no need to reflect further. A disciplined seeker is ready to see, to listen, and to receive, noticing new options and solutions. We can look for companionship as we explore the mysteries of life. As seekers in the world, we can be less anxious about confusion because we have learned that it can be useful. To seek with awareness, intention, and less anxiety will in turn open our eyes to ever more possibilities.

Susan had been a member of a spiritual discernment group in her congregation for several years. She had occasionally been a seeker with her group. She later described how the Prayer Model had helped her to be a more effective seeker in other situations. For a few years, she was struggling with a chronic illness that limited her ability to get out of the house and hold a job in the profession she had successfully practiced for years. She felt isolated and lonely and often thought that God was ignoring her prayers for a more fulfilled life. As Susan reflected on her situation, she began to clarify for herself what was bothering her about being confined to home most of the time. She then began to look at what she could change about her home life to make it more satisfying.

Susan realized that her dilemma was not really about being confined to her home but that she needed to be more creative about managing her home life to provide for what she needed and wanted. She was able to reflect about how this change in focus had helped her to see how God was present to her in ways she had not seen before. This seeker had been able to explore more deeply because she had been a seeker in her discernment group. Her participation in the Prayer Model continued to bear fruit even though it had been a couple of years since she had met with the group.

THE RESPONDER

The role of the responder can be a challenging one. I (Catherine) remember how nervous I was the first time I sat in the chair of the responder. What would I say? How would it sound to everyone? Would I make a fool of myself? I could compete with these other responders and give the best response! Surely, I could come up with some advice for the seeker that would fix everything! Surely, I would have an answer or could solve the problem! I wanted to sound wise and insightful. The role of responder seemed like a performance, and I was anxious about what others might think of me. The performance anxiety caused nervous butterflies in my stomach.

One of the first things a responder can do to perform the role more faithfully is to release that performance anxiety which comes from anticipating a negative judgment from those who hear what you have to say. The responder should trust in what the Spirit has to say through him. No one—not even the responder—can judge a response because each response is only one piece of the puzzle. No one can see the whole puzzle, so who can say whether the piece the responder provides is wise or useful? Even the seeker may not fit that puzzle piece into the picture for a while. Therefore, it is useless to make any sort of judgment about a response or for others to judge it. Although letting go of performance anxiety may be a challenge at first, performance anxiety is a waste of energy and a distraction. The best remedy for performance anxiety is to be faithful to the process and learn to trust the Spirit.

There are two fundamental responsibilities of the responder—companionship and listening. Companions come together to encourage each other along the way. A companion is present by being sensitive to the other's needs, providing objective feedback, being a sounding board, or just listening. The responder's presence in itself conveys care and support. The seeker is surrounded by people who are intently listening to what she is saying and feeling, who walk each step of the journey with her. The seeker knows that she comes to this circle of prayer and is heard. One who is heard is not alone. This is perhaps the greatest gift that the responder can offer—to be a companion by listening and hearing.

In the Prayer Model, participants re-create themselves and each other in the act of listening. The seeker is listened to intently and surrounded by her companions who are trusted with some of her most intimate thoughts and experiences. Being heard like this is a rare opportunity in our culture, which is more often about the self rather than the other. This presence can be a great comfort in a time of trouble or can add to the celebration in a time of joy. The care and support demonstrated by the listening circle provides the seeker with a time and place to be open and vulnerable, and vulnerability and openness lead the way to transformation. Of course, listening is valuable to the responder as well, who practices listening skills and receives information, both of which have the potential to be transformative in the responder's life. Participants journey together and teach each other.

Companionship and listening shape the presence of the responder, who is also charged with providing a verbal response. The responder might think of the response as a gift to the seeker—a piece of the puzzle to help complete the picture that the seeker is trying to put together. The gift could be one of observing the seeker and reflecting back what has been observed. Like holding up a mirror, the responder comments on what he heard and observed while the seeker was speaking. Perhaps the responder can describe a moment when the seeker became more animated or joyful or deeply sad. The responder may have noticed that the seeker repeatedly used demonstrative body language, such as shaking a finger or grimacing in reference to a particular character or encounter of the story. If the seeker used a particularly strong word or phrase or repeated a word or phrase, it may be helpful to note this. The responder can reflect back something to the seeker in a number of ways that will help the seeker grow in self-awareness or learn how she is being perceived by others. The responder may wish to offer the gift of an image or a passage from scripture or poetry that connects in some way to what the seeker said. Perhaps the seeker's story reminds the responder of a parable or a psalm. During the silence, an image such as the strong oak in Psalm 1 or

Noah's rainbow might come to mind for the responder and may serve as a metaphor for the seeker. The seeker could gain insight from any of these.

The responder's gift may be a question that could help the seeker clarify his or her thinking. A useful question can also help the seeker break free from black-and-white thinking and explore unimagined possibilities. A responder might ask, "What was your experience of the Spirit in this situation?" or "How do you imagine your life when this situation is resolved?" or "What is your deepest desire in these circumstances?" Sometimes a good question can help a seeker see options that were not apparent before.

One thing a responder must do is refrain from giving advice. Responders will feel especially tempted to give advice if the seeker's story resonates with personal experience and they have survived a similar dilemma. Giving advice distracts the seeker from her dilemma and shifts her focus to the responder. As a responder, if you are tempted to give advice and can offer nothing else, it is best to explain that you are unable to respond in a useful way and pass to the next responder. The Prayer Model is not designed for giving and receiving advice but rather for companionship. If a seeker really does want advice, he may say so and ask for it directly. However, even when it is requested, the responder should resist. If a seeker truly wants advice, it is appropriately sought in other settings.

The responsibility of the responder is not to advise or fix the other, give answers, or resolve the other's problems. The desire to fix, provide an answer, or resolve a problem for the seeker reveals more about the responder than anything else. What the responder shares may eventually lead the seeker to some resolution, but resolution is the work of the seeker, not the responder.

One time I (Sandy) was serving as a responder for a group. As the seeker spelled out his story, I felt myself becoming restless as I recognized that I had lived through something very similar. I was also remembering how grateful I was that I had arrived at a very satisfactory resolution for my dilemma. I found myself feeling increasingly eager to tell the seeker my story and about my solution. I wanted to save him from having to undergo the same distress I'd been through.

During the silence, I was aware that I had to put my own personal feelings aside in order to be faithful to the role of responder. The point was not to rehearse my own story and tell him what to do, tempted as I was to do exactly that. The seeker's story resonated so deeply with my own experience that any response I could offer would be clouded by my personal feelings of confusion in that moment. I came to the realization that I simply was not able to put aside my own story and solution.

When it came time for me to respond, I told the seeker that I was reluctantly having to take a "pass" at that time. I explained to him that this had nothing to do with him or what he had said. I said that I was too involved in my own "stuff" and that I simply was not able to remain objective and be truly open to what the Spirit might be offering right then.

Even when responders and compassionate observers get drawn into some of these common snares, the Prayer Model and Spiritual Discovery Method have much to offer. With practice, participants learn to recognize traps more readily and to avoid them. But even when we fall right into them—and we all do from time to time—the process works.

The Responder in the World

As responders continue to practice giving responses, they may discover many skills and disciplines they wish to develop. One of the skills the responder can practice is listening. Since we are required only to listen while the seeker is speaking, we can practice the skill of listening with the whole heart. This is not something that our culture trains us to do, and we do not often seek out the opportunity to practice this kind of listening. We can be better responders to the world and to others when we have learned how to listen without the distraction of conversing. We can learn to listen with singleness of heart and mind, with all of ourselves—body, mind, and spirit. Responders can also practice listening to how the Spirit speaks, listening to that image of God within, to the desires of the heart, and to our own wisdom. A good listener is sorely needed in our world and is a great gift to others. Those who are privileged to be listened to so thoroughly may be transformed by that experience in itself, finding that they are not alone in their struggles and that someone else cares at least enough to truly listen. Good listening skills are often appreciated and valued in our talkative culture. Many resources are available for those who wish to develop listening skills, but most are focused on skills needed for listening to others in conversation. The Prayer Model provides the opportunity to explore and experiment with many dimensions of listening.

The power of listening becomes clear as the responder practices it. A good listener can be a healing presence in the world. Sometimes being heard is all that a speaker needs in order to move on. A good listener can take what he hears and translate it for others. One of the learnings for the responder is how much more the world needs listeners than advisers and fixers. Of course, we do need advisers and fixers, people who can imagine how problems are solved and goals accomplished. But it seems we have many fixers and advisers, and comparably few listeners.

If we can notice how we listen to and wait for the Spirit to speak within the prayer, we may recognize parallels to how we wait in the world. We may discover that we wait patiently or impatiently, peacefully or anxiously, or that we find the act of waiting to be boring or stimulating. We can pay attention to what we are waiting for and any expectations that we may have. Are we optimistic or pessimistic? Do we expect that truth will be revealed and that the Spirit is present? These attitudes and postures reveal how open we are to the work of the Spirit within us. If we can slow down enough to observe ourselves with compassion, we may be surprised by what we find. If we wait expectantly and anticipate the movement of the Spirit, the Prayer Model allows us to open up a spaciousness within that makes room for what will come. Waiting with openness and anticipation, expectation of the presence of the Spirit, and awareness of surroundings can be very useful in the world. Waiting is a worthwhile discipline to learn to do well.

Another spiritual life skill that the participant learns in the responder's chair is to respond to others and to the world with detachment. This way of responding is different from debate, argument, or self-revelation, when we may be invested in establishing our identity or getting others to see our point of view. A detached response is one that we offer freely, with no expectation of the one who receives the response. For example, a responder might talk about Psalm 121 and be thinking about how "I will lift up my eyes to the hills" can be an image of hope. The seeker may imagine instead that the hill is high and God seems far away. The responder understands that God will use what she offered in a way that she may not understand. A responder who offers her gifts to the world with no strings attached, no expectation of the one who receives it, is free to let go of the offering. If we can learn to offer our responses and let them go, we will begin to discover that our happiness no longer depends on what someone else will do. We are free from dependence on others. We can then learn what it means to be detached in other situations. Likewise, when we become detached from our responses to the world, we let it go with no investment in what happens to it. Detachment is a spiritual skill that surprises and refreshes the world.

Responders may also begin to see the power of questions in the world. A few good questions here and there can lead to transformation. A good question can draw factions away from either/or thinking and lead to compromise. An insightful question leads to exploration and discovery or to clarity of thinking. A useful question can also help individuals break free from black-and-white thinking, exploring unimagined possibilities and seeing new options. The world needs questions so much more than it needs answers. Answers end conversations, questions begin them.

THE COMPASSIONATE OBSERVER

The compassionate observer sits silently throughout the prayer process. She is not required nor given an opportunity to speak. Although this role may appear to be quite passive, the compassionate observer has several assignments to fulfill.

One responsibility of the compassionate observer is to hold the sacred space. In the Prayer Model, the compassionate observers form the outside circle, creating a "container" which prayerfully holds the speaking and listening of the inner circle. What is said and heard there stays within the circle and is understood to be spoken in the context of a sacred trust that is respected and honored by all. This container creates a uniquely safe time and place where participants are able to speak freely. The essential work of the compassionate observers assures the safety within the container.

Another responsibility of the compassionate observers is to listen. With their gift of listening, the compassionate observers encourage the seeker and responders to speak freely. Like the responder, the compassionate observers listen with the whole self—body, mind, and spirit. They hold what they hear in prayerful silence. Whoever speaks can be assured that their words will be heard. The listening of the compassionate observers is deep and all-encompassing.

Since the compassionate observer is required *not* to speak, she has the luxury of listening without the responsibility of forming a verbal response. This frees her to attend to listening to the speaker and the Spirit. The compassionate observer is entirely free from the pressure of speaking. Rather than being confined by not being able to speak, the silence of the compassionate observer is liberating. The compassionate observer is free to listen as the Spirit guides the reflection. The freedom can often lead the compassionate observer to surprises and insights for her own spiritual journey.

I (Sandy) was leading a group that was new to the Prayer Model, so I served as timekeeper. As the responders were beginning to offer their responses to the seeker, one of the compassionate observers began to speak. She was eager to talk about what she thought the Spirit was communicating through her. I gently reminded her that this was the time for the responders to speak and that compassionate observers were to remain in silent prayer. She seemed surprised and bewildered but remained silent.

Later, during the debriefing, the compassionate observer who had wanted to speak told us how eager she had been to share her insights with the seeker. It seemed to her that the requirement to remain silent was shutting out what she believed the Spirit might be speaking through her. She went on to say, however, that she had been surprised when one of the responders offered something very similar to what she had intended to say. She had come to understand that all the group members had been instruments of the Spirit and recognized that if an insight was important, the Spirit would convey it in the Spirit's own way, in its own time and place. Someone else in the group said that even if no one had verbally expressed the compassionate observer's insight, the Spirit could be trusted to convey it if the Spirit saw fit to do so.

The compassionate observer who is compelled to speak during the Prayer Model may be struggling to let the Spirit be in control. This struggle is sometimes verbalized when the compassionate observer questions whether it is her own desires that she follows or the Spirit's. Is she hearing the Spirit or is she fooled by her own inner voice? This is a false distinction. It is not an either/or question but rather a matter of sorting out the many voices within and discerning which one originates from that image of God that is within each of us. Rather than understanding inner voices and desires as something to be tamed or conquered (or controlled), they can be viewed as something to be discovered. Participants *let* the Spirit speak rather than trying to *make* the Spirit speak. As an instrument of the Spirit, the Prayer Model can be trusted to provide an opening for the Spirit to speak. It provides the opportunity to practice tuning the "ears" to that inner voice which arises from the image of God within. Instead of struggling with the Spirit for control, participants join with the Spirit and learn to recognize the Spirit's voice.

The Compassionate Observer in the World

The role of the compassionate observer is learned and understood primarily through practice and application. This is true for all of the roles, but it is especially true for the compassionate observer because one learns by not doing something—not speaking. Because she does not speak, the compassionate observer is free to listen. By not speaking, the compassionate observer can pray for the others. Because she does not have to speak, she can create sacred space. In addition to listening and creating a sacred space for the prayer, the compassionate observer can practice acute perception and non-judgmental observation. Like the other roles, these powerful practices can be taken into the world every day. Compassionate observation can be practiced in the world by remaining silent and listening rather than stating opinions. *Compassionate* observers can observe what is happening in the world while withholding judgment. This can lead to being more informed and realizing greater possibilities and options. They can consciously take the practice of compassionate observation into any situation. The role of compassionate observer is one that brings many challenges and rewards to a spiritually attentive person. In part 3, we will explore in depth all that the role of compassionate observer offers.

THE TIMEKEEPER

Even for the timekeeper, the Prayer Model offers opportunities to practice spiritual disciplines. The role of timekeeper is primarily one of guidance, directing the group through the steps of the Prayer Model. This requires offering some gentle verbal direction along with signaling the time with the prayer chime. Since the timekeeper also acts as a compassionate observer, all the opportunities that are there for the compassionate observer are available to the timekeeper. It is difficult, however, for the timekeeper to be fully present to the compassionate observer role because he must pay attention to the responsibilities of the timekeeper. He remains outside of the prayer to some degree in order to serve and guide the group. For this reason, it is especially important that the role of timekeeper be rotated among the group members.

As the first step of the Prayer Model, the timekeeper leads the group in a spoken prayer. The opening prayer should be brief and general. Its purpose is to focus everyone's attention and to open everyone to the presence of the Spirit. Offering one or two sentences might seem an insignificant task, but this assignment is an important one because it sets the tone for what is to follow. If the pray-er is not careful, an opening prayer can reveal her agenda for the session. It would be inappropriate, for example, for the timekeeper to say something like, "God, help our seeker to follow you into missions where Jesus has called her to be a servant to the poor." The timekeeper's agenda in this example is obvious, but sometimes agendas can be very subtle and prayer can be used to influence others.

Occasionally, the timekeeper must ring the chime while someone is still speaking. But when everyone in the group comes to trust the prayer process and allows it be what it is, no one will take offense if the timekeeper rings the chime in mid-sentence. Group members are urged to keep in mind that this is appropriate and to accept that what needed to be said was said.

In order to maintain the order of the prayer, the timekeeper must sometimes redirect a participant who inappropriately speaks out of turn. Maintaining the order of the prayer is important for several reasons. One reason is that the prayer order creates a predictable, reliable structure that the participants come to trust. They know when they will be speaking, when they will be listening, and when they will be in silent prayer. Participants can prepare themselves to be listening or speaking. No one needs to be surprised or wonder what the next step will be. This predictability allows participants to be more focused and attentive to the present moment. Another reason to maintain the prayer order is that modifications to the prayer impair its effectiveness. They can be distracting. After learning the prayer order and becoming comfortable with it, participants can begin to go deeper into the experience and develop the skills described in this chapter. Confusion about the prayer order may also result in a breakdown of the process, leading to ordinary conversation rather than an intentional rhythm of silence and speaking. The opportunity to develop listening and speaking skills may be lost.

In our experience, the Prayer Model has been shown to be effective in making room for the Spirit to speak and, in turn, making it possible for participants to be more open to whatever the untamed Spirit may offer. Any breakdown in the structure immediately begins to dilute its effectiveness. So if a compassionate observer or a responder speaks out of turn, the timekeeper can quietly say something like, "This is the time for the seeker to speak" or "Your gift is one of compassionate silence." The timekeeper then guides the group back into the process at the point where the order was interrupted.

During the debriefing for one group, the timekeeper, Tom, had plenty to say about serving in that role. He said that he had accepted the prayer chime and then, as the group sat down in its circles, wondered what on earth he had signed up for, because he felt totally unprepared to do the job. Someone had handed him the outline for the prayer order, so he had taken a deep breath and plunged in. Tom said that he had felt inadequate to carry out the job of timekeeper and at the same time to be a compassionate observer, when all he wanted to be was a compassionate observer. Then, when one of the compassionate observers started to speak and his role as guide for the prayer required him to remind the person that she was to maintain silence, he felt uncomfortable redirecting her. As he continued to reflect, Tom said that the experience had led him to a new appreciation of the prayer order. But he also admitted that he was very glad that the job of timekeeper rotated and that he wouldn't have to do it again for a long time.

The Timekeeper in the World

As the one who guides the group through the prayer, the timekeeper practices skills that can be useful in the world. One of these is assertiveness, which might be called for during the prayer. One time, a timekeeper stopped the group in the middle of the prayer because someone walked into the room. She explained to the intruder that the group was in the middle of a confidential prayer process and politely asked him to leave. The timekeeper also practices assertiveness when she redirects participants who speak out of turn. Although this can be uncomfortable at times, gentle firmness can be helpful in any relationship, and this practice in the prayer helps participants to be more comfortable with it in other situations.

Sharing leadership among peers is a particular gift of the Prayer Model as members accept both the responsibilities of leadership and the discipline of following. This is a setting in which tolerance and acceptance develop, and each member of the group can confront the challenges presented by the timekeeper role. As participants experience the responsibility of redirecting a peer in order to keep the group on track and the discomfort that goes with "correcting" a group member, they can empathize with each other. They have had the same experience. Group members, as they recognize the value of shared leadership, may take the practice to other groups.

The personal presence of the timekeeper can also be developed in the Prayer Model. The pace of the prayer gives the timekeeper opportunity to notice and reflect on her presence as a leader. Tone of voice, posture, pace of speaking, and other aspects of a prayerful presence can have an effect on the group, though it may be quite subtle. For example, a calm demeanor may help an anxious seeker to relax. By contrast, an anxious leader may distract participants or spread tension in the group. The timekeeper has an opportunity to develop some self-awareness of how her presence affects a group, which is then useful in other life situations.

CHOOSING A ROLE

Group members select a role at each prayer session. As the group comes to the prayer circle, participants choose which role they would like (except for the seeker's role, which has been prearranged). It is wise for participants to choose among the roles so that they experience each one regularly. The group is enriched by the variety of participants in each role. Alternating between roles serves the needs of the group by providing a listening presence, responding presence, and a seeking presence.

The role of the seeker requires particular attention. Generally, it is best to self-select this role ahead of time. Each time the group meets, the seeker for the next session can volunteer. This gives the seeker plenty of time to gather and organize his thoughts, and be open to new insights. It also provides time for the seeker, within the given situation, to act as a seeker and work at developing an open, inquiring presence. Keep in mind, however, that it is important for the seeker to remain flexible and make adjustments if he finds his presentation changing even as he offers it. Sometimes seekers are surprised to discover a more needful issue emerges at the last moment. However the seeker engages the role, sitting in the seat of the seeker is a privilege as the seeker is the center of the group's focus and the process often results in a deep spiritual learning.

If they are aware of areas within themselves in need of spiritual development, participants can select the role that not only serves the group but also addresses those areas. Should a participant notice that she finds herself in the same role every time the group gathers, she may wish to examine her motives. What is drawing her to this role? What might she be resisting or avoiding in the other roles? She may then decide to sit in the place that makes her most uncomfortable. She can learn a great deal in each place when self-awareness and openness guide her choice. For example, an introvert may want to challenge herself and volunteer to be a responder. An extrovert may wish to work on his listening and practice of silence by taking the place of a compassionate observer. Another member may want to practice resisting the urge to fix others' problems by choosing the responder role with the specific intention of offering some alternate appropriate gift. If a participant wants to work on becoming less judgmental, she may elect to sit in the chair of a compassionate observer where she can notice her judgmental thoughts and choose to take a less critical view. The place of the timekeeper may be a good fit for those who wish to practice assertiveness. Even a well-practiced life skill can use some renewal from time to time.

Choosing a Role in the World

One who has practiced the roles in the Prayer Model may choose among them when she is in the world. She may choose to be a listening presence, responding presence, or a seeking presence. This choice may be made based not only on how she can best be present to others but also based on what she believes she needs to learn. At times, it is important to choose to be a compassionate observer in order to be a listening presence. At other times, a verbal response is called for. Sometimes a situation can be served by taking on the role of seeker who wonders aloud about possibilities and ponders options.

Each role provides a particular means of the Spirit's presence. Members of the leadership council at St. John's, for example, found that they had more effective conversations with church members as they improved their skills of listening and responding. They were able to gently but assertively redirect a conversation, moving it away from gossip or correcting misperceptions. They were able to be compassionate observers in the congregation and began to develop a keener sense of some of the underlying dynamics that were at play. They found that as they chose and practiced the roles in the prayer, they became more effective at choosing and practicing those roles in the larger congregation. They were able to choose a role that they thought was needed rather than to react without thinking. Even their skills as spiritual leaders were enhanced. As the council developed the discipline of the prayer, the congregation in turn continued to benefit not only from thoughtful leadership but from healthier interactions. The Prayer Model was sacred yeast in the community.

The roles also provide opportunities for participants to work on particular areas of their own lives. If a participant finds that she is often reactive to a family member, for example, and this reactivity prevents her from listening to what he may have to say, for a while she may choose the role of the compassionate observer when she encounters him. She may discover that her compassionate, silent presence begins to decrease her reactivity and opens up the possibility for listening. It may take some time or require her to return to her group and practice compassionate observation in the Prayer Model again and again. When reactivity is replaced by compassionate observation, a situation can be transformed. Another participant may realize that he is often giving unsolicited advice. When he recognizes how often he does this, he also acknowledges that when he tries to stop giving advice, he doesn't know how else to respond. When he returns to the Prayer Model, he may wish to take the responder's role where he will have an opportunity to practice responding in ways that do not include giving advice. Eventually, this person may be able to let go of his tendency to give advice and respond to others with more understanding.

Participants in the Prayer Model can consciously choose to take on a role in a given situation. They can discern how a certain role might be useful or see how their own presence can be more effective when it is shaped by the role they have chosen in that moment. Each of the roles—seeker, responder, compassionate observer, and timekeeper—offers gifts and skills that can be called upon when they are needed.

Chapter Five

The Order of the Prayer Model

As the foundational component of the Spiritual Discovery Method, the Prayer Model is most effective in a community when it is faithfully practiced. Adhering to the order of the Prayer Model is critical as it enables participants to be present to the self and to each other at each moment of the prayer. The participants engage in one activity at a time, each for a specified period and in a particular order. The full attention and intention of each participant is desired at each step of the process. The seeker speaks, listens, and reflects in turn—one activity at a time. The responders listen without being required to prepare a reply. They take time for reflection and speaking, focusing fully on their present responsibility. The compassionate observers are free to be present as they pray and listen. The model provides the opportunity to practice wholehearted attentiveness and intent at each step in the process.

The opening prayer offered by the timekeeper should be just a sentence or two, setting the appropriate tone. It is general in nature, focusing on opening the heart and mind, fruitful listening, gratitude for the group, or the presence of the Spirit, for example. The timekeeper should avoid setting an agenda or stating an opinion, praying in words that avoid making assumptions about the seeker and her discernment. Statements like "Help Sally to let go of her pain" or "Help us to guide Sally through her troubles" hint at what Sally should say, how she should feel, or how she should deal with events in her life. This also implies that Sally needs to be "fixed."

The first three minutes of silence allow participants to be mindful of the process and the presence of the Spirit. They can let go of whatever might be a distraction for them and give their attention to the prayer. Everyone does this in her own way, but this might include quieting the body and finding a comfortable posture, breathing deeply, or opening the heart. Participants may pray silently for the seeker, the whole group, or to hold the sacred space.

During the seeker's sharing, the responders are focused and listening. The seeker may have prepared some notes to follow along as he presents but also remains open to changes to his presentation as the Spirit guides him. Throughout the prayer, compassionate observers are listening, praying for the group, maintaining the sacred container through prayer, or noticing their own thoughts and feelings.

In the following three minutes of silence, responders pray about what the Spirit wishes to say through them. They should be aware of how the seeker's presentation may have affected them and should be attentive to letting go of anything that may actually be advice. The seeker may be collecting himself if he is emotionally overwhelmed or may be praying for an open heart and mind to receive what is offered.

While the responders are speaking, the seeker does his best to listen and be open to what is being said. This is a time to trust that he will receive what is needed from the responses. The compassionate observers may wish to pray for each responder as he or she speaks and for the seeker as he listens.

During the next three minutes of silence, the seeker may be sorting through responses, reviewing and integrating them, and looking for insights. This is only the beginning of a process that may take weeks or months, so the initial impressions and understandings are all that is possible here. The responders and compassionate observers may pray for the seeker, notice what is happening for themselves internally, and continue to hold the sacred space.

The seeker then speaks briefly, offering a summary of what was heard, a reaction to something that was said, or a reflection on how the responses were related to each other or how they resonated with his own experience. Sometimes, the seeker may simply wish to thank the responders.

The final period of silence can be a time for participants to continue their prayers for participants and the process, to reflect on what they heard during the prayer that might be useful for themselves, or to silently offer prayers of thanksgiving. The final "Amen" closes the prayer and signals a transition into the debriefing.

The prayer order provides a predictable setting for spiritual exploration. For example, participants may discover that they can remain focused for three minutes of silence. But if invited into an undetermined period of silence, they might become distracted and anxious, wondering when the silence will end. Accustomed to the predetermined and familiar period of silence, the prayer order enables them to remain attentive to the Spirit.

The safety of the prayer order allows for greater spiritual risk-taking. The seeker can be more open and discover how deeply she has been affected by her situation. The confidential nature of the circle allows a seeker to speak with a depth of feeling that may not be safe in other settings. She can then begin to go deeper in exploring those emotions and responding to them. In the prayer order, participants may enter into unfamiliar spiritual arenas, which can be engaged with less anxiety because they are approached from within the safe and familiar boundaries of the prayer.

CREATING ORDER IN THE WORLD

The Prayer Model creates an opportunity for orderly attentiveness to the Spirit. In what is often experienced as a messy and chaotic world, singleness of heart and mind focus spiritual exploration and enable participants to listen and wait for the voice of the Spirit. With a structure in place, participants are invited to let go of any anxiety they might have about the unpredictable nature of the Spirit and the world. This then enables them to listen more effectively to what the Spirit may say to them in the moment. The conscious structure of listening and speaking or compassionate observation creates a space in which one can keep from being overwhelmed by disorder.

The chaos and messiness of the world can be noticed but not permitted to interfere with listening to the Spirit. If we can choose to create a structure around our attention to the Spirit in the Prayer Model, we can also choose to put some parameters on how we listen to the Spirit in the world. For example, I (Catherine) had an experience with a young woman who was struggling to redefine her faith. She had come to believe that the teachings of her childhood church were no longer satisfying her spiritual curiosity and the reality of her life. But she was afraid to leave her church and search for another spiritual home. She felt like she was losing her faith. It was just too overwhelming. We discussed the opportunity to explore this transition in her life while permitting her to put some "order" around the process. Perhaps she could take small steps into this faith transition by visiting new congregations while returning to her old church as often as she felt she needed to. She could think in terms of maturing in her beliefs rather than betraying or losing them, thus understanding her transition to be natural and orderly progress. She could take time to be her own compassionate observer and note without judgment her thoughts and feelings. She could also remind herself that she had companions with her on this journey. There was no need to jump into what appeared to her to be overwhelming chaos when some structures and orderly ways of thinking could frame her experience. As she began to bring some order to her transition, this young woman was able to listen to the Spirit more effectively.

We can also bring order into the chaotic world through our interactions. The participant who recognized she was being reactive with a family member chose instead to be a compassionate observer in the relationship. Over time, she noticed she was becoming less reactive and more able to listen. Unable to goad her to react to him, the family member became less provocative. Both the participant and her family member changed. Her skill as a compassionate observer was brought to bear on a challenging relationship, and the relationship was changed.

Participants in the Prayer Model discover the value of order as they pray together. They may then work to bring order to their relationships and their own inner spiritual processes. Intentional periods of seeking, responding, and observation bring some order into situations that may seem chaotic and overwhelming. This allows participants to let go of fears and anxieties and wait for the Spirit to speak rather than react or retreat.

Chapter Six

A Modified Prayer Model

As Jane Vennard describes in her foreword to this book, some years ago she organized a small group of colleagues who were seeking support in their ministries as spiritual directors and counselors. The group gathered once a month to reflect on their work, discussing practical matters such as insurance, training, and boundaries, and maintaining accountability to ethical and professional guidelines. In the process, they also guided each other in spiritual reflection on events in their personal lives, which they found especially meaningful. Both of us (Catherine and Sandy) have been a part of the group for all or most of the nearly twenty years it has been in existence. We have consistently made use of Jane's Prayer Model as described in this book and, over time, have discovered the many benefits it offers.

Several years ago, Jane participated in a workshop led by Quaker spiritual leader Parker Palmer, where she was introduced to open, honest questions. Jane brought the concept back to our group, proposing that we try it out as we continued our practice of the Prayer Model. We agreed and since then have come to greatly appreciate the advantages of open, honest questions. As a result, we frequently use them in our group sessions.

In this modification to the Prayer Model, after the seeker's presentation and the period of silence comes a fifteen minute period of open, honest questions from the responders. The seeker verbally reflects on each question. Thus, the prayer order becomes (asterisk indicates a strike of the chime):

Brief opening prayer
*Three minutes of silence
*Up to ten minutes for the seeker to present

*Three minutes of silence

*Fifteen minutes of open, honest questions from the responders and ver-
    bal reflections by the seeker

*Three minutes of silence

*Each responder has up to two minutes to offer a gift

*Three minutes of silence

*Seeker takes up to three minutes to share closing thoughts

*One minute of silence

*"Amen"

It is important that the seeker always has the option of inviting open, honest questions from the responders or using the original Prayer Model. When the seeker invites open, honest questions, she also allows herself time to reflect, thus setting the pace of the questions. Responders also allow moments of silence between a seeker's verbal reflection and the next question. The seeker may also choose not to answer a particular question. Following these guidelines maintains a gentle pace and helps create an atmosphere that prevents the process from becoming an interrogation.

Formulating open, honest questions requires careful consideration. There are several temptations to avoid. The first is approaching the questions from the perspective of the questioner's needs rather than those of the seeker. Even asking for more detailed information about the situation, for example, displays this tendency as it reveals the questioner's needs. The questioner must avoid allowing his or her own agenda to influence the questions. This applies specifically to a desire for fixing the situation or advising or saving the seeker. The questioner's opinions about the situation are not sought or welcome. The questioner must be wary of any tendency to hint at an opinion or to disguise an agenda in a question.

Open, honest questions should be short and to the point. They are aimed at eliciting the seeker's own assessment of the situation. At encouraging the seeker's contemplation of her thoughts and feelings about the situation. At inviting exploration in ways the seeker may not have considered before. At going deeper into the seeker's own wisdom about the situation. One way to formulate questions that accomplish these aims is to be sure that the questioner has absolutely no investment in what the answer to the question will be.

Asking open, honest questions takes some practice and is learned with experience. Sometimes the difference between appropriate and helpful questions and inappropriate questions is subtle. When asking open, honest questions, it is helpful for the questioner to attend to her intuition. Even if a question seems strange, she should trust it. Such a question may have an unexpected effect. Another time, it may be wise to sit with a question if one is hesitant. With experience, participants will begin to trust their intuition and learn to recognize authentic open, honest questions.

For example, if the seeker is wrestling with a difficult friendship, an open, honest question might be, "What would this relationship look like if everyone was reconciled?" or "If this relationship was never reconciled, how would it affect the way you think about yourself?" A responder would not ask, "Doesn't this situation make you angry?," but rather, "How do you feel about this situation?" A responder would not want to make a suggestion by asking, "Don't you think you should get out of this friendship?" Instead of asking "Do you think your friend is being unfair?," which limits the seeker's thinking and reveals an opinion, one would ask "What do you think about what your friend has done?" or "How do you feel about your friend?" Open, honest questions invite the seeker to expand his thinking.

The use of open, honest questions is advised for groups that are familiar with the original Prayer Model and have regularly engaged in seeking, responding, and observing. Participants who have practiced the disciplines of listening, observing silence, and seeking self-awareness, trust, and compassion will be better prepared to formulate open, honest questions. Familiarity with the original Prayer Model and its disciplines provides a firm foundation for taking on the practice of this challenging variation.

The addition of open, honest questions in the Prayer Model introduces another skill that participants can take into the world. The use of open, honest questions in everyday conversations can introduce intriguing elements into such encounters. For example, asking questions that invite people to think more deeply about what is going on personally for them in a situation rather than focusing on the behavior of others can have unexpected results. Open, honest questions invite us, as everyday seekers, to think creatively and imagine new possibilities.

In his book *A Hidden Wholeness*, Parker Palmer reflects on his own experience as a seeker when he says that he is most grateful for an open, honest question that "invite[s] my soul to speak and allow[s] me to hear it."[1] By its nature, an open, honest question encourages a thoughtful response. An open, honest question trusts the seeker to look within for guidance. One who asks open, honest questions does so based on the conviction that "everyone has an inner teacher whose authority in his or her life far exceeds my own."[2]

Donna was the leader of an adult spiritual formation group that was familiar with the Prayer Model and used the Spiritual Discovery Method to structure meetings. The group had faithfully practiced the method for several years and had become skilled as seekers, responders, and compassionate observers. Group members exhibited a profound understanding and appreciation of the method. Donna thought the group might benefit from taking the next step and adding a period of open, honest questions to their practice of the Prayer Model.

At the group's next meeting, Donna explained how open, honest questions could be added to the Prayer Model. She handed out a summary of Palmer's description of open, honest questions and discussed it with the group. Then group members experimented by composing questions. After some practice, they began to understand the qualities of an open, honest question and how to create one. With a little more discussion, the group decided they would like to try adding open, honest questions to their prayer time. At future meetings, the seeker would have the option to choose the model without the questions or to add the questions.

The next month, Jim was the seeker. Jim had already decided that he wanted to try the open, honest questions. He thought it would help him go deeper in exploring his spiritual dilemma. For several months, Jim had been wrestling with what to do about a long-time friend whom he felt had betrayed him. This friend had taken credit for some writing that Jim had done. Although the betrayal seemed obvious to Jim, the friend seemed unaware of any problem. Jim wrestled with how to reconcile. It had been a painful experience for him, and he felt stuck.

As the group gathered for the Prayer Model, Jim took his place as seeker. When it came his time to speak, he described the situation with his friend. He talked about the broken trust and how painful it was. He wondered how this friend could be oblivious to what she had done and could never have imagined this friend as unfeeling or lacking integrity. Jim expressed his anger at his friend and his guilt about being unable to forgive the betrayal.

When the time came for open, honest questions, one responder asked, "What metaphor would you use to describe this situation?" There was a moment of silence as Jim thought about it and took his time responding to the question. There was more silence before another responder asked, "Where is there light between you and your friend?" Again, Jim allowed himself time to reflect on the question. Another asked, "What makes you hopeful?" Jim's reflection and answer followed, and the first responder spoke again, asking,

"What do you need for healing to happen?" Finally, Jim was asked, "How is God present between you and your friend?" The period of open, honest questions ended—eight questions in all—and the group went into silence.

The group finished the Prayer Model with gifts from the responders, Jim's closing thoughts, and the final period of silence. The group moved into a larger circle for the debriefing, and Jim shared his experience of the Prayer Model. He appreciated the gentle pacing of the questions. He felt that the questions had been asked with compassion and that they had certainly caused him to consider more deeply his own thoughts and feelings about the situation. He was also aware that some of the questions would require further reflection on his part over the days and weeks to come. He would be searching deeply within himself for the necessary strength and wisdom for dealing with the relationship. Jim had found that the open, honest questions helped him renew his efforts to heal the relationship. For the first time in weeks, he felt hopeful that this was possible.

Chapter Seven

Debriefing

Debriefing is the opportunity a group takes following the Prayer Model to discuss with one another the experience its members have just shared. This is not a time for recapping or furthering the substance of the discussion the group has undertaken. Rather it is an occasion for reviewing the group experience as well as the individuals' assessment of their participation in it. The graceful simplicity of the Prayer Model allows each participant a unique experience, bringing his own spiritual questions. Debriefing the experience helps each participant see how others engage the experience in unique ways, thus expanding his own thinking and, in turn, engaging the prayer more creatively and openly.

At the same time, members of a group may learn that they have a common experience of the prayer process. This discovery can serve as a comfort in time of crisis or a confirmation in uncertainty. For example, participants may see that everyone noticed the same distraction or found the prayer especially intense. I (Catherine) once debriefed with a group that engaged in the prayer while a choir was rehearsing nearby. Several participants said that it enriched the experience rather than being a distraction. Discussing the prayer process may help members be open to a variety of experiences when they observe how others enter into the process. The common prayer journey of the group can be a gift to each participant.

The debriefing provides an opportunity for self-examination, both for the group as a whole and for the individual. In discussing what happens in the process of the prayer, participants take note of how the prayer creates openings for the Spirit of God to move in their midst. The quality of the experience can be discussed and any unusual dynamics noted. A group may realize, for example, that they are worried about an absent member and discuss how that affected their prayer time. Or perhaps some are tired that day, and they examine how that changed the quality of the experience. Groups can celebrate those things that contributed to a positive experience and remedy those things that detracted from it. One might leave the prayer experience having discovered something about herself that makes it difficult for her to be open to the Spirit. She can follow up by praying about it and may choose to come to the next gathering with a more open heart and mind.

Another outcome of debriefing is to ensure the Prayer Model functions smoothly. This is a time to discuss any misunderstandings of the model, miscues, or difficulties, such as not being able to hear or something about the space that is distracting. Adjustments can be made in response to what is learned in the debriefing. Success with any discipline grows when participants pay attention to practical matters. The debriefing provides a time for the group to do that.

DEBRIEFING IN THE WORLD

Life is full of moments and events that can benefit from debriefing. As participants become familiar with the discipline of debriefing in the group, they can encourage the practice in other groups. For example, if a meeting space is new to a group, they may wish to discuss how the space works for them or what they may change. Or a study group might discuss how well they have followed their schedule and how it worked for them. Healthy groups are attentive to the logistics of meeting spaces, times, and agendas and make improvements or changes from time to time. Such groups also encourage the identification of otherwise often unspoken dynamics. A leadership council, for example, as it concludes its meeting, may take time for each person to say how he or she is feeling. This can be formative for the group. Becoming aware of others' thoughts and feelings enables participants to examine their common experience and respond appropriately.

TAKING THE PRAYER MODEL INTO THE WORLD

A member of the council at St. John's Church described how her experience on the council had changed her life. Because she had practiced the Prayer Model and participated in decision-making on behalf of the congregation, she had developed the habit of intentionally reflecting on her own significant life decisions and taking them into prayerful discernment. Sometimes she imagined herself as a seeker preparing and presenting her dilemma to a group. She incorporated periods of silence into her prayer and listened for the Spirit. She took more time to settle on a decision and noticed that she had become less fearful about taking risks. Overall, she reported less anxiety when making significant decisions in her life. She appreciated the skills and disciplines that she had learned in the prayer and was grateful that her participation in the Prayer Model had been a transformative experience.

Regularly practicing the Prayer Model with a group provides a time and place to focus on spiritual growth and learn new skills that can be taken into the world. Each individual participant will discover new and uniquely personal opportunities for growth. As we have explored each role, we have noted the particular disciplines that can be developed in that role. The many spiritual skills that are learned and practiced transform participants from within and, in turn, transform the participants' relationships and interactions. After practicing a new way of listening in the prayer, for example, listening in the world is improved. After learning an intentional way to seek, participants see how seeking can be transformed in their own lives. When a responder lets go of how the seeker uses her response, she can let go of what the world does with what she offers to it. A compassionate observer may realize that she is comfortable listening and holding a difficult conversation in a sacred space. Timekeepers discover that they can effectively redirect a conversation with gentle assertiveness. Skills such as listening, detachment, and seeking—along with all the many other skills that the prayer encourages—change how a group member engages the world. Whatever the topic or situation, the *way* of interacting has changed.

As participants grow in self-knowledge and become more aware of their own desire for spiritual growth, they can go deeper into prayer and discover even more opportunities and possibilities for growth. The spiritual practices described here are just the beginnings of what can be learned and practiced in and through the Prayer Model. In the years of practicing this model, we have found that it has never exhausted the possibilities for spiritual learning and growth.

The Vennard Prayer Model is a powerful tool by itself, but as the foundational component of the Spiritual Discovery Method, it significantly transforms the process of decision-making. All the skills, processes, and practices of the Prayer Model provide an arena for listening to the Spirit and the wisdom of the group members as they come together in prayerful discernment. Having examined the Prayer Model in depth and seen how it can transform groups and individuals and be taken into the world, we now turn our attention to the Spiritual Discovery Method.

II

The Spiritual Discovery Method

The longtime pastor of Christ Church had just retired, and the board of trustees began the process of calling a new pastor. Because of financial constraints, the congregation could only afford a part-time pastor. About half of Christ Church's board members were of the opinion that they should explore the possibility of merging with another congregation rather than calling a new pastor. They thought this would be a responsible and realistic way to proceed, since funds were so tight, and they saw it as a creative and life-giving possibility. But other board members had characterized the merger group as "unfaithful" and "unwilling to work at it," so some people who wanted to explore the merger option were a bit hesitant to voice their opinions. About half of the board said they should proceed with calling a new part-time pastor and then grow the congregation, hoping to increase income and make a full-time pastor's salary manageable. This group thought other options, such as merging with another congregation, would compromise the identity and history that had formed this community that they loved so much. They said that joining with another congregation was "taking the easy way out" of a difficult situation. To them, a merger seemed like failure. The board found that they were divided into two strongly opposed camps.

As they began gathering data from the members of the congregation, they realized that the congregation was also evenly divided about the direction they should take. The board knew this question of calling a pastor versus merging needed to be resolved before moving ahead, and they decided from the beginning that they should bring an intentionally prayerful approach to their decision.

The board of trustees at Christ Church were familiar with the Vennard Prayer Model, as it had been used by various groups in the congregation in recent months. They also had used it as they individually had discerned about participation in the board. So they began each of their meetings with the Prayer Model, followed by a discussion about all the facets of the decision that was before them. Gradually, the board brought more people into the decision-making process, inviting members of the congregation representing divergent views to join the board's prayer sessions. These visitors took the role of seekers, describing their own thoughts and feelings about the point of view they represented. The visiting seekers would join with the board in the Prayer Model and then participate in the following discussion time. After several months, board members agreed that they thought they had prayerfully heard all the viewpoints.

Board members had collected the data they thought they needed and had explored the process of congregational mergers. They had examined the financial circumstances and other factors that determined if they could survive as an independent congregation. They believed that all the pros and cons had been carefully examined. It seemed, however, that they could not agree on whether to call a part-time pastor or merge with another congregation. At this point in the discernment process, things seemed to have stalled. Board members found themselves rehashing previous discussions rather than moving toward a decision.

As the board continued to work at coming to a decision, they realized that some difficult things needed to be said and nobody seemed to want to say them. Aspects of the conflict had been buried beneath the facts and figures. At one meeting, an observant council member took the place of the seeker and wondered out loud if those who favored the merger had been fairly heard. He asked if they felt their point of view had been mischaracterized or even if they felt personally attacked. He wondered if some hurt feelings were not being acknowledged. His questions were just what were needed to move the group into a deeper conversation. The board agreed that it was worth the time and effort to address these relational issues before continuing their discernment process.

The difficult work this required paid off as it elicited the very best of those who participated. Members found that they grew to trust each other more deeply. By the time they completed their work of reconciliation, the board found that they could discuss the conflict in the congregation more honestly, with less reactivity, and with more compassion for each other. People were less defensive and more open. They found they were able to listen to and explore new options.

Members of the board who had advocated for calling a new pastor and growing the church began to see things differently. Through all of the prayer sessions, research, study, and discussion, they had begun to see how a merger might be a positive move for the congregation and even that it might be a more realistic option for them. They could now see that the Spirit might be leading them toward merging with another congregation, rather than remaining on their own. The view of those who had held the merger position had begun to look courageous rather than the "easy way out," as they had previously thought.

The board arrived at a decision to explore merging with another congregation. They put together a plan to inform the congregation of their discernment. Although they believed that members of the congregation who had hoped for calling a new pastor might be upset by the decision, they found that many of them were also more open to new ideas and had begun to realize that the merger was what the Spirit was guiding them to do. It appeared that through the prayerful process in which the board had included a number of them, trust had grown and the community had been strengthened. Not only had the board members grown in their trust of each other, they had earned the trust of the congregation. They were now in a strong position to move ahead with planning for the merger.

The board of trustees of Christ Church created an environment in which the congregation could come together for the purpose of making an important decision in a spiritually grounded way. The Prayer Model and discussion time helped members develop trusting relationships, listen carefully to each other, and respond thoughtfully. They were able to explore creative options that they probably would not have considered before. They invited congregational members to be a part of the process by joining them in this method of spiritual discernment. The process set the tone and provided the structure for their decision making. The congregation used the Spiritual Discovery Method to guide them through a crucial time in their history.

The Spiritual Discovery Method consists of the Vennard Prayer Model followed by a period of discussion and exploration. In a decision-making process, a seeker might present his thoughts or feelings about any aspect of the decision, and although his presentation is often not the focus of the exploration time, it may shape the discussion or help participants to have a fresh perspective. The Prayer Model also sets the tone of the discussion, helping participants to speak intentionally and listen carefully. The use of the Spiritual Discovery Method provides a prayerful structure for any communal decision-making process in which participants wish to include spiritual discernment.

In part 2, we will provide a definition of discernment followed by a description of the Spiritual Discovery Method. Essentials of group life are described, demonstrating how they contribute to the success of the method, and are followed by some cautions about challenges to the success of the method. This is followed by a commentary on how the method can be transformational for individuals, groups, and congregations as they develop the spiritual skills and disciplines that are offered in the group experience and take them out into the world.

Chapter Eight

Discernment

To discern is to come to a decision or conclusion about something. The decision or conclusion itself is not the main concern here, but rather the process by which we go about making the decision. We are always engaged in a process of decision-making, so paying attention to how we arrive at decisions will help make possible more thoughtful, well-discerned decisions.

The Spiritual Discovery Method necessarily incorporates a spiritual dimension in the process of discernment. Describing the idea of spirituality quite broadly, theologian Joann Wolski Conn offers three definitions:

> Spirituality is understood as a contemporary philosophical and psychological as well as religious term. Philosophers speak of our human spirituality as our capacity for self-transcendence, a capacity demonstrated in our ability to know the truth, to relate to others lovingly, and to commit ourselves freely to persons and ideals. Psychologists sometimes use the term for that aspect of personal essence that gives a person power, energy, and motive force. Religious persons speak of spirituality as the actualization of human self-transcendence by whatever is acknowledged as the ultimate or the Holy, that is, by whatever is considered religious. [1]

Danny Morris and Charles Olsen, authors and leaders in the field of spirituality and community, address the topic of spirituality more precisely when they describe a process of spiritual discernment as "see[ing] the heart of the matter with spiritual eyes; from God's vantage point, see[ing] beneath the surface of events, through illusions within human systems, and beyond the immediate and transient." [2]

Conn's definition refers to the spiritual *source*, a source that is drawn upon by discerners and which she identifies as 'the ultimate" or "the Holy." Throughout our book, we refer to that ultimate spiritual source for discernment as "Spirit" or "Spirit of God." Morris and Olsen focus on the *process* of spiritual discernment when they describe it as seeing "with spiritual eyes" and doing so "from God's vantage point." Thus, spiritual discernment is a process by which we endeavor to approach decision-making from God's vantage point and to do so with spiritual eyes. All the while, we acknowledge the Spirit of God as the primary agent in that discernment process.

A spiritually grounded decision-making process requires participants to pay attention to the presence of the Spirit and what the Spirit has to offer. It is rooted in prayerful listening to the Spirit. It rests on the knowledge that the Spirit of God is present at all times, in all places. The Spirit does not need to be invited; it is already present. Discernment is about taking notice of how the Spirit is present and active. The Spiritual Discovery Method builds upon awareness and attention to that presence in all things and at all times.

The process of discerning draws on a range of authorities. Sometimes spiritual decision-makers look beyond themselves, consulting sacred texts and wise counsel, praying for wisdom and guidance from the Spirit, and taking into particular consideration the needs of others. Spiritual decision-makers also look within themselves, examining their personal desires and interests, being mindful of their gifts and abilities, and looking for a sense of inner peace about a potential decision. All spiritual decision-makers, at one time or another, may use all of these types of authorities in a discernment process. Participants also find some authorities have greater appeal in different situations and that the decision-making process grows and changes as group members grow and change.

In a discernment process, different authorities may appear to conflict with each other. For example, the personal desires of the seeker may lead to a discernment conclusion that conflicts with the given realities of the situation in which she finds herself. The seeker might experience a strong call to travel abroad for a mission trip, but the necessity of being at home with her young children prevents her from responding to that mission call. The process of group spiritual discernment is about sorting through such conflicts and weighing the authorities while trusting that we all do our best job of discerning when we resolutely attend to what the voice of the Spirit has to say.

People bring various paradigms that shape their process of discernment. Some are confident that God has a specific and detailed plan for each and every person. For them, discernment is about discovering God's plan and then doing their best to align their decisions with that plan. Others believe that God has a broad hope and vision for them. They discern by relying on scripture or advice from a wise elder. These are examined in the light of common sense, personal desires and interests, with the goal of shaping a plan that is consistent with what they understand to be God's broad hope and vision for them. Others seek an intimate relationship with God in order that their sense or knowledge of God will lead to decision-making that is in accord with God's individual desire for them. Still others are guided in their discernment by certain overarching values, such as love or harmony, and they will seek to shape their decisions in conformity with those values. We encourage groups to identify and acknowledge these assumptions because of their significant influence on the discernment process, both for the individual and the group. The Spiritual Discovery Method allows for and welcomes all of these paradigms for discernment. Each approach adds to the richness of the process.

There may be times when group members are confused or challenged by the various paradigms that others bring as they participate together in the discernment. The person who is confident that God provides a specific plan may annoy the one who begins with overarching values and urges the others to shape their decision based on them. Another may seek to resolve a dilemma by citing passages from sacred scripture. The one who consistently reminds the others of the practical realities may be confronted by another who appeals to the others to "pray for inspiration." Acknowledging these differences while agreeing to listen closely for the guidance of the Spirit will be helpful when such confusion or challenges are encountered. Participants will discover that their diversity has been a blessing to their discernment.

Members of a community encourage and support each other in their listening. Sometimes this calls for confronting one another. For example, if a seeker is impatient to act on what she has discerned, group members may urge her to slow down in order to receive further clarity. They promise to stay with her as she continues her discernment. If someone seems to be minimizing an obstacle, the others can help her realistically evaluate the situation. The community may assist others in avoiding unrealistic thinking while at the same time encouraging the consideration of options they may not have imagined.

One's companions bring their own lifetimes of experience to the discernment. The collective listening and wisdom of the group is a significant asset to any discernment process, helping group members to see where they can be more open, attentive, and receptive to the Spirit's voice. Those who practice spiritual discernment in community recognize how influential the others are to their discernment process. One participant described the benefits of engaging in discernment in community this way: "Other people have different angles and points of view on an issue and bring to the table things we by ourselves wouldn't see." In a community, each person, as a unique vessel of the image of God, will hear and transmit an original way of understanding the Spirit's wisdom.

Chapter Nine

Group Administration

FORMING A GROUP

When forming a new group for the purposes of engaging in communal spiritual discernment, potential members will benefit from learning about spiritual discernment and the purpose and goals for their particular group. They will also be helped by understanding something of what to anticipate from the spiritual discernment experience and what will be expected of them as participants in the spiritual discernment process.

Prior to gathering the group members for their first meeting, they should be encouraged to read this book to learn about the Prayer Model and the Spiritual Discovery Method. It will be helpful for them to makes notes about what attracted their attention as they read the chapters and, more importantly, what questions came up for them as they read about the model and the method.

Next, convene the group for a general discussion about the Prayer Model and the Spiritual Discovery Method, based on the group members' reading and their identification of highlights and questions from their reading. The group should estimate a time frame for the discernment process they are entering into, along with setting the duration and frequency of the meetings. Most essential will be coming to a common agreement about the group's purpose and work, as well as its goals.

Once potential members have a solid understanding of what they are agreeing to do, each person should take the necessary time to reflect on their desire and availability to be a part of the group and the discernment process.

Although group members may need some time and experience of the method to fully understand what a commitment to a spiritual discernment group means, self-awareness and careful consideration of their commitment is important before joining a group and will be worthwhile for everyone in the long run. For instance, everyone is better off if a potential member is aware of her own time or energy limitations and declines at the beginning rather than joining and later dropping out. Everyone is honored when all potential participants engage in this preliminary discernment. Members will find they all have a higher quality experience if they are committed to each other and to the process and, in the end, will enjoy fruitful discernment.

MANAGING THE ADMINISTRATIVE DETAILS

Groups should manage the administrative details of the process so that they don't become a distraction. A lack of communication may be a problem, for example, when participants are not sure what time a meeting begins or where to find the gathering place. The significance of other administrative details may not be as obvious, but they are just as important. Participants might need to be informed about materials that should be reviewed for the next meeting or items to bring for a ritual. Poor administration of the details may become disruptive to the work of the group. Good administration will contribute to the ability of the group to focus on the discernment process.

Groups need to decide together how they will manage the details of administration. An administrator would attend to such needs as scheduling, communication, refreshments, and record keeping, although administrative needs will vary depending on the purpose or task of the group. Sometimes, choosing an administrator is straightforward. For example, a congregational leadership council usually includes a person who attends to administrative details. When the council uses the Spiritual Discovery Method, the same person may continue to serve the same purpose throughout the discernment process. Often within groups there are people who are gifted in and enjoy administration and may be the natural choice of the group to see to these responsibilities. Some groups may need to negotiate these roles.

The meeting place should be chosen with both the Prayer Model and the Discernment Method in mind. A place most conducive to the method will provide a space where the group can conduct the Prayer Model and then have a different space to come together for break and discussion. If only one space is available, the group will need to rearrange their chairs and equipment after the Prayer Model. For the discussion, for example, the group may gather in an open circle or around a table if participants are referring to books or recording notes. The group may want an easel with newsprint or electronic devices, such as computers or audiovisual equipment. The discussion space should serve the purpose of the group, just as the prayer space supports the Prayer Model.

Some groups will benefit from having a facilitator, who may receive compensation for her services. A facilitator has some expertise that would be useful to the group, such as a spiritual director who guides a group that is new to the idea of communal discernment. A facilitator may be responsible for organizing, scheduling, setting up the meeting space, and other administrative duties. Facilitators may teach discernment skills, lead prayer exercises, and guide discussions. A youth group, for example, already has a leader who is gathering the group, setting meeting times, and recruiting new members. He may also serve the group as teacher, spiritual guide, worship leader, or counselor. In this case, he is already serving the group as both facilitator and administrator. The work of a facilitator will vary according to the needs of each group. The facilitator should be familiar with the Spiritual Discovery Method.

Chapter Ten

The Design of the Spiritual Discovery Method

The Vennard Prayer Model is the foundation of the discernment process. Because group members have listened deeply during the prayer, they are more skilled at listening as they discuss discernment questions. Because they have practiced seeking as individuals, group members are better able to clearly define and articulate their discernment question. Each component of the method is affected by the fact that the group members pray together. The success of the method depends on the consistent practice of the Prayer Model at every gathering of the group.

The Spiritual Discovery Method gathering begins with check-in time so participants can make the transition from daily life into the group life. Next comes the Prayer Model, followed by a short break. This break allows the group to move to the exploration and discussion activity. The method ends with an intentional closure, so that participants can shift back into daily life.

The two main components of the Spiritual Discovery Method are the Prayer Model and an exploration and discussion period. The flow of the meeting goes like this:

Gathering time
Prayer Model
Break
Exploration and discussion
Closure

The Prayer Model along with the exploration and discussion take up most of the meeting time. The gathering, break, and closure times should be brief and loosely organized, though they should not be skipped or conducted haphazardly as they are critical to healthy group life. Transition times allow group members to informally strengthen relationships among themselves.

The group may begin with a prayer or brief ritual. The gathering time should include an opportunity for each person to check in, limiting this to two or three minutes per person without interruption or conversation. One purpose of this check-in is to allow participants to leave behind whatever might be engaging their attention and energy so they are able to participate fully in the group meeting. The total time allotted for gathering should be limited to thirty minutes.

The break between the Prayer Model and discussion may include refreshments and should take about ten to fifteen minutes. Following the discussion, a short ritual may be used to close the session. This may consist of a simple prayer or a blessing passed among members.

Meetings of the spiritual discovery group take between one and a half to two hours and are generally held once a month. The intervals between meetings provide an opportunity for the Spirit to work. In addition to reflecting on the group discernment, the time between meetings provides an opportunity for participants to reflect on their own spiritual journeys and work on spiritual skills. For example, if a participant realizes that she is being judgmental as a compassionate observer, she may spend the month noticing when she becomes judgmental and practice letting go of her judgments. The spiritual growth that takes place for those who practice the method doesn't happen only during the group meetings.

EXPLORATION AND DISCUSSION

The content of the exploration and discussion time within the Spiritual Discovery Method will be shaped by factors such as the task of the group and the organizational setting. For example, a leadership board such as Christ Church's may need to discuss the mission and vision of the congregation. At St. John's, the council needed to discuss recruitment. A vocational discernment group, such as the one that helped Philip examine his vocational questions, would want to get to know the person discerning the vocation. Later, as this group redefined its purpose and began to work on spiritual formation, they chose texts to explore. Any kind of decision, dilemma, transition, question, or topic can be the focus of the exploration and discussion.

THE PRAYER MODEL IN RELATION TO THE EXPLORATION AND DISCUSSION

The Prayer Model and the discussion and exploration time are related in that they are both integral to the spiritual discernment group's purpose and goals. As group members, faithful to the design of the method, work together to arrive at a spiritually-grounded decision, both the Prayer Model and discussion time are critical to the overall discernment process and help move the group toward that decision.

The Prayer Model is the foundation for the Spiritual Discovery Method. It establishes the spiritual climate for the discussion and exploration. The overall results for the entire session can be surprising. Kathy, a seasoned discernment group leader, said that when the Prayer Model was used in the first half of a gathering, it "set the tone for the entire session." She went on to describe what happened in the second half of a meeting that had begun with the Prayer Model: "The second half is more peaceful, more thoughtful, more respectful, responses are more deliberate, and people seem to be more present to each other." The results for the entire session were that the participants seemed to "listen better, look for more careful solutions, and honor differing points of view more thoughtfully" than when the Prayer Model had not been the first part of the meeting.

An imperative of the Prayer Model is that the content of the prayer not be discussed outside the Prayer Model. Participants need to trust that what was shared in the prayer is held in sacred confidence, not to be discussed beyond the Prayer Model. There is one exception to this requirement in that the seeker herself may choose to reopen a topic from the Prayer Model during the exploration and discussion part of the meeting. A discussion of the topic the seeker brings to the prayer may be appropriate and useful for the entire group. Only the seeker can give permission for the content of the prayer to be discussed in any context outside of the Prayer Model.

Although the content of the speaker's presentation is not to be discussed during the exploration and discussion, the issue or issues identified by her presentation may be discussed in broader and more general terms. For example, the board of trustees of Christ Church welcomed a seeker who expressed her fears about a possible merger with another congregation. The board's discussion and exploration, which followed, were about preparing for changes that they realized would be inevitable if there was to be such a merger. Philip brought his job dissatisfaction to his discernment group's Prayer Model, and the subsequent discussion and exploration were more generally about the pros and cons of continuing education. The council at St John's invited a seeker who was discerning her gifts for leadership, and then explored the qualifications for leadership that might be most needed in a congregation. The seeker's presentations are often deeply personal and at the same time provide opportunities for discussion and exploration of related but broader topics.

Only the seeker can permit the content of her presentation to be discussed outside of the prayer. This boundary makes vulnerability possible and creates trust within the group. Even when there is no obvious relationship between the topic of the Prayer Model and the topic of the discussion and exploration time, the prayer significantly influences the discussion by creating a more peaceful, thoughtful, and respectful tone.

Chapter Eleven

Essentials for the Spiritual Discovery Method

Essentials for the Spiritual Discovery Method are those foundational princi-pals that help spiritual discernment groups function smoothly and come to a decision. To assure a satisfying and fruitful discernment, groups should fa-miliarize themselves with these essentials. Group members' personal com-mitment to these essentials is fundamental as participants will depend on each other to observe them and will hold each other accountable to them. From time to time, group members can renew their commitment to these essentials by reviewing them and evaluating the group's success in each area.

The essentials are as follows: defining the discernment question, main-taining confidentiality, attending to group dynamics, seeking consultation and communicating appropriately outside the group, managing time, utilizing ritual, planning closure, and speaking the truth in love.

DEFINING THE DISCERNMENT QUESTION

Effective communal discernment requires that members of the group have a common understanding of the question they are discerning. As they begin to consider their discernment question, they may be surprised to discover a number of different understandings about what it is. At this point, the group must discuss it and come to agreement about the question.

In order to formulate a discernment question, the group must undertake some necessary groundwork. First, determine what precisely is known of the situation for which the discernment is sought. This will most helpfully involve fact-finding and outside consultation. Next, articulate and explore the various options that might provide a solution to the dilemma. Then, narrow the choices to two or three. Finally, compose the question based on these clearly described options. The question should be focused enough in scope for the group to manage within the time frame of the discernment process as well as to lead to an actionable decision.

The discernment group at Christ Church carefully formulated their question: "Should the congregation seek to merge with another congregation or call their own part-time pastor?" They had laid the groundwork by examining their needs and resources and had agreed that these were their two choices. Had they begun with a question such as "What is the next step for Christ Church?" without doing the preliminary fact-finding and consulting about their options, their discernment process may have been vulnerable to distraction and possible derailment. One group member might have found herself wondering if they should hire a pastor-search consultant. Another might have been praying about reaching out to the neighborhood in order to build up the congregation. A third might have been pondering what characteristics they should look for in their new pastor. If they had failed to focus their discernment question, the Christ Church group may have ended up discerning what kind of pastor they were looking for while leaving unresolved some fundamental questions, such as what they could afford and whether they were truly in a position to call their own pastor.

A well-defined discernment question is important because it also results in an actionable decision. Once the Christ Church board decided to seek to merge with another congregation, the next steps were clear and indicated some immediate goals, so they knew what to do next.

MAINTAINING CONFIDENTIALITY

Maintaining confidentiality is vital to building and maintaining trust in a group. For example, when a seeker tells his story to the group, he must be able to trust that no one will pass it along. Because the group will be talking about personal and sacred things, confidentiality is a personal and sacred trust. Even if the seeker's story is well known or common knowledge in the community, participants must not discuss it outside the group. A seeker's story is his to tell—no one else's.

Keeping confidentiality in all components of the method's design, from check-in to closure, is particularly important for groups using the Spiritual

Discovery Method. The relationships that develop because confidentiality is secure enable one to speak one's deepest truths. A seeker who is as honest as possible with himself and with others will gain the most from the process, as his humility opens him to the Spirit's direction. Such a seeker is able to accept new directions without self-recrimination and with hope. This seeker, revealing the deepest truths about his dilemma, also provides responders with helpful information for their own reflection. The collective wisdom of the group grows with more information and deeper truth. The discernment process is more productive when decisions rest upon foundations of truth. Confidentiality enables truth to be revealed.

In their commitment to maintaining confidentiality, group members may appear secretive to others outside the group. If they decline to discuss the discernment group, this could appear to be secret keeping and may be destructive. They may create a cliquish impression and cause unnecessary hard feelings. People outside the group may wonder why group members are withholding information about the group. Since spiritual discernment is not commonly practiced or understood, a spiritual discernment group may appear quite stand-offish and mysterious.

Confidentiality is not the same as keeping secrets. In response to questions about a discernment group, participants may openly comment on the processes involved without disclosing confidential information. They may describe how the Prayer Model works or how often the group meets or who the participants are. They may not, however, discuss the content of the discussions, such as a seeker's story or how a decision was reached. Confidentiality is healthy and builds trust, while secret keeping is unhealthy and can create barriers.

ATTENDING TO GROUP DYNAMICS

Group dynamics consist of the relationships and behaviors within a group. These relationships and behaviors can be positive and healthy, or unhealthy and destructive. Keeping confidentiality, for example, is an example of positive group dynamics. Another example of positive group dynamics would be clear and thorough communication among members.

One task of a new group is to create norms. Norms help a group maintain positive group dynamics. Each group can create its norms to suit its particular situation, but the first and most obvious norm should be the confidentiality requirement to which everyone must agree. Members may wish to ensure everyone understands who will handle administrative responsibilities, or how often the group will meet, and what preparation is required. Groups may ask everyone to buy into expectations about punctuality, how seekers will be scheduled, or other similar housekeeping details. Norms should be clearly understood, everyone should agree to them, and they should be revisited occasionally. All of the group members are responsible for maintaining the norms and may be required to speak up when a norm is being violated.

Problems with group dynamics can often be subtle or difficult to manage. What does a group do if the same member arrives late each time and interrupts the Prayer Model? How does a group respond to someone who only attends about half the meetings? What if confidentiality is broken? Issues such as these will be addressed below.

CONSULTATION AND COMMUNICATION

Sometimes a group needs to communicate with people who are outside of the group. For example, leadership councils such as those at St. John's and Christ Church need to report their progress or decisions to the larger congregation. Other groups such as a vocational discernment group may wish to gather information from outside experts. A group may find that they have encountered an obstruction to their process and seek objective consultation and assistance.

I (Catherine) once worked with a group that was doing some vocational discernment with a member of their congregation. Over months of coming together in prayer and discussion, the group began to get lax about practicing the Prayer Model. At some meetings, they skipped the model entirely. After a couple of meetings without the model, one member challenged the group by describing what she observed: without the prayer to set the tone, their discussions had occasionally devolved into acrimonious debate, and they had stopped listening to each other. The group members agreed that they had gotten off track and thought it might be wise to get some objective feedback about the situation. Together, they wrote a brief description of what had happened and appointed a spokesperson to contact me to make arrangements for a consultation.

We began by talking about how and why the group had stopped praying together. We examined the dynamics of the debate they were having and how they had strayed from their original focus on discernment. They realized how important the Prayer Model was to the success of their process and the way the neglect of their prayer discipline had adversely affected their exploration and discussion. They resolved to renew their commitment to the method and agreed to include the Prayer Model in all future meetings. We reviewed their norms and agreed that they were adequate and that the group should be more attentive to them. Although the situation had been difficult, they agreed that they had learned from their mistakes.

Group members also agreed that they felt good about the process they followed to communicate beyond the group and call in a consultant. With the full knowledge and agreement of each person in the group as well as input from each member, the communication outside the group honored confidentiality and was transparent. Although the group was not functioning at its best, no one felt betrayed or blamed, and each took responsibility for what had happened. They were thankful to the group member who had called them to account for their neglect of the Prayer Model. Because the group had addressed their issue openly and with everyone's participation, trust was strengthened. They were grateful that each person had contributed to the successful resolution to their problem.

When communication beyond group members is required, it should be done with the full knowledge and agreement of the entire group. Prior to any communication outside the group, members should be aware that the communication will be taking place, who will be contacted, and who will be responsible for initiating the contact. Each member should participate in determining what will be said or made public. Each group member should also have an opportunity to contribute to what is communicated. Any communication beyond the group should be done thoughtfully and openly.

MANAGING TIME

Time is one of the significant elements of discernment. Making a decision takes time, and most decisions benefit from being afforded sufficient time and care. Ample time allows more opportunity for the Spirit of God to work within the hearts and minds of those who are discerning. Time taken for prayer and reflection will make room for the Spirit to participate in all phases of the discernment process. It will provide decision makers the occasion to slow down and listen for the voice of the Spirit.

When a group comes together to do discernment, making time for communal prayer, listening, imagining, reflecting, exploring, and discussing is essential. Ample time makes possible a more thorough examination of various possibilities and outcomes. The tendency to rush the process should be resisted. As participants agree to join a discernment group, they make the commitment to take the time the discernment process requires.

Group members should be aware of how well they are managing the time as the discernment process is progressing. If the group begins to reexamine what has already been accomplished or group members become bored and urge the group to move ahead, these are signals that time is not being managed well. Time management may also be a problem if group members feel rushed or think that issues are being overlooked. Groups will benefit from periodically reviewing how far they have come in their process and what remains to be explored. At the same time, they need to make sure they examine all the topics that will inform their decision. The groups should seek to strike a balance between the desire to move ahead and the necessity to be thorough.

However, the time will come when the work of discernment is finished. The discernment process is ready to conclude most obviously when the group reaches a definite decision on the question they have undertaken to discern. Some groups may hesitate to conclude their work, even when there is consensus, because the decision that has been reached is perceived to be painful for some who will be affected by it. For example, if a group is discerning how their congregation will restructure its ministries, any suggested changes may lead to disappointment on the part of some who are passionate about their current ministry. Decisions usually result in change, and change may be hard for some. The discernment process however must end, so the community may take action on the decision.

Some decisions are time sensitive. Circumstances may require firm deadlines. In this decision-making process, the group may be able to use the Method only for a few meetings. The skills learned and practiced in the Spiritual Discovery Method can be effective when transferred to a necessarily quick decision-making process. If a group has practiced discernment using the Method, they will gain enough experience to make such decisions well. Even when time is short, such decisions can be held in silence and prayer, explored, and discussed.

UTILIZING RITUAL

Throughout history, human beings have ritualized and celebrated occasions such as meals, moving into a new home, and life transitions, such as births, graduations, marriages, and deaths. Rituals build relationships and help shape a group's identity. They may be composed of words, actions, or both. Groups come together to practice ancient, well-known rituals, or they create rituals of their own. Some individuals have private rituals they practice regularly. Discernment groups may find their communal experience enriched by including rituals in the life of the group.

Rituals include the use of symbolic props, gestures, and words. A ritual may be as simple as lighting a candle at the beginning of a meeting and leaving it burning throughout. Perhaps a prayer is recited as the candle is lit and extinguished. Groups may create a greeting ritual to do as they come together or a sending ritual as they disperse. They may write a blessing for the seeker or create a ritual for the whole group that symbolizes openness. A leadership council might keep a symbol of their congregation in a visible place as a reminder of who they are and what they are about.

Groups can decide for themselves what they wish to emphasize in their work by surrounding it with ritual. They can create their own rituals and then allow them to evolve. Groups can choose their words and actions by starting fresh or borrowing from other rituals. The use of rituals in the Spiritual Discovery Method can enrich the experience, mark transitions in the group, and keep groups mindful of the sacred nature of their work.

PLANNING CLOSURE

The time will come when a discernment group concludes its work and discontinues its gatherings. Perhaps the discernment question has been resolved or group members are no longer available for meetings. Whatever the case, the ending of the group should be intentional. It should be planned and celebrated in some way. Groups are encouraged to decide how they will celebrate their life together.

They could gather for a meal or a worship service. Telling stories about the group experience and what it has meant to each group member would be appropriate for such an occasion. They could create a closing ritual. The closure does not need to be elaborate, but should be planned collaboratively to celebrate the achievement of their purpose as well as to honor and complete their time together.

SPEAKING THE TRUTH IN LOVE

Writing to the early Christian community at Ephesus (in present-day Turkey), the apostle Paul describes what is required in order to create faithful, wholesome, and healthy communities:

> But speaking the truth in love, we must grow up in every way into him who is the head, into Christ, from whom the whole body joined and knit together by every ligament with which it is equipped, as each part is working properly, promotes the body's growth in building itself up in love. (Ephesians 4:15–16 NRSV)

Paul is asserting here that the virtuous community is one that is made up of parts of a body that are all "working properly" and "[promoting] the body's growth." Such a community is one in which each member discerns his function and faithfully lives into it. In this community, members speak truth to each other in love.

The first part of Paul's directive is to speak the truth. This is vital for a group of people entering into communal spiritual discernment. In order to do that successfully, it is important for the group to be watchful for manifestations of two different and even contrary tendencies of human beings. The first is avoiding speaking the truth, whether out of fear of hurting another or being seen as unloving. At the other end of the spectrum is taking pride in being the one who always "tells the truth," no matter the consequences.

The second part of Paul's injunction to speak the truth consists of the requirement that it be spoken in love. Widely read author Frederick Buechner elaborates on this critical component of speaking the truth in love: "To tell the truth in love means to tell it with concern not only for the truth that is being told but with concern also for the people it is being told to."[1] In other words, truth-telling takes into consideration not only the truth itself but lovingly attending to all the parts of the body at all times, most especially the other or others to whom the truth is being spoken.

Truth telling begins with love. The most faithful and fruitful discernment takes place in this kind of loving and truthful community. In the Spiritual Discovery Method, participants benefit when they begin on the solid ground of the truth. This solid ground provides the group with a communal understanding of the facts as they begin the decision-making process. No single member has more of the truth than another. The decision-making process is most effective when it begins with the present reality and progresses from there. A traveler must begin with "You are here" in order to decide which way to go. Throughout, speaking the truth in love continues to keep the process from devolving into fantasy. A decision based on fantasy can lead to unrealistic choices.

The journey must begin with self-knowledge. Although truth may be difficult to hear at times, its clarity makes visionary transformation possible. In a community of love where the trust level is high, truthful feedback is most able to be spoken and heard. What better place is there to hear difficult truths about ourselves than within a circle of people who love us? Within that circle of love and truth the most effective and life-giving discernment takes place. The Spiritual Discovery Method functions most effectively within such a circle and is designed to create and sustain this trusting environment.

In order for the spiritual discernment community to succeed at achieving the most effective and life giving discernment, its members must speak the truth and do it in love. In other words, truth and love exist collaboratively, each making the other possible. Speaking the truth in love promotes the growth not only of the individuals in the community but the community as a whole. Finally, the group members will discover it is in such a community, where love and trust levels are both high, that the truth is most able to be spoken and heard.

All of the essentials described above contribute to a positive group environment, which then supports the discernment process. Clearly articulating the discernment question, keeping confidentiality, paying attention to group dynamics, knowing when and how to communicate outside of the group, managing time, utilizing ritual, planning closure, and speaking the truth in love will each help build up the group and strengthen trust. All these essentials will contribute to strong and healthy relationships within the group and the group's discernment will be most fruitful.

Chapter Twelve

Challenges Groups Encounter

Groups using the Spiritual Discovery Method may experience certain challenges. Some occur more frequently than others. These challenges are broken confidentiality, attempts to influence the outcome, preparing to be vulnerable, challenges with group dynamics, time pressures, group members "disappear," lack of accountability, and the belief that the discernment process "fails."

BROKEN CONFIDENTIALITY

Perhaps the most devastating challenge for a spiritual discernment group is broken confidentiality. In the course of the prayer and discussion, participants may reveal some of their deepest and most personal thoughts about themselves and their spirituality. The rule of confidentiality applies to all components of the method, including check-in, prayer, break time conversations, discussion, and closure. Each member is required to honor the sacred trust that the group maintains. Broken confidentiality may be irreparable and could destroy a group.

A congregational spiritual discernment group had been meeting for a year or so with Rose as an active participant. Group members had come to trust each other, developing very positive relationships among themselves. At one of the group's gatherings, Rose shared the deeply personal spiritual struggles she was experiencing as a result of her breast cancer diagnosis. Although her medical condition was commonly known in the congregation, she had been very private about her spiritual struggles.

Several weeks later, a woman who was not a group member approached Rose. She told Rose that she knew about Rose's struggle with spiritual issues over her cancer and that she was happy to know she had someone to talk to about her own breast cancer. Since Rose had not shared her spiritual struggles with anyone except her group, she realized that someone in the group had told the woman about them. She felt betrayed and wondered whether she could even continue to participate in the group.

Rose found a way to talk about her dilemma in a conversation with Tom, one of her good friends and a member of the group. Tom urged her to consider sharing what she had told him with the whole group. He thought her departure would be a serious loss for the group. Although Rose was hesitant, with Tom's support she agreed to do that. The group meant a lot to her, and dropping out would have been very difficult for her too.

At the next meeting, Rose took the place of the seeker during the prayer, telling the group what had happened and how hurt and angry she felt. She described how difficult it was to share with them and to talk about what felt to her like a betrayal. She told them how much they meant to her and how she valued the relationships with everyone. She also admitted that continuing with the group would be very difficult for her.

As they left the prayer and regathered for their discussion, Rose gave permission to talk about the content of their prayer time. With tears in her eyes, group member Debbie confessed that she had spoken to the woman who had approached Rose. Debbie went on to say that she had only shared that Rose was struggling spiritually but had not discussed any details of Rose's situation. Debbie had wanted the other woman, who also had breast cancer, to know she was not alone in her struggles. Since Rose's cancer was well known in the community, it had not occurred to her that Rose's spiritual wrestling was confidential. It had been a thoughtless mistake, and Debbie felt terrible about it. She asked Rose to forgive her. She said that she could see how the whole group was affected by what she had done and asked forgiveness of the group as well. Debbie, indeed the whole group, now had a better understanding of what it meant to be confidential. They would all be more careful in the future.

Through this experience the group members had an opportunity to recommit to their promise of confidentiality. Everyone saw the effect that broken confidentiality had on one of their members and on the entire group. They deepened in their understanding of what it meant to maintain confidentiality and were now determined to be more intentional about how they talked to others about the group. They were also much more aware of how important it was to be able to trust each other. Though Rose's experience had been a painful lesson, group members felt that they had grown closer as a group, building on their strengthened commitment to each other. Because of Rose's courage, a potential crisis had been turned into an opportunity.

ATTEMPTS TO INFLUENCE THE OUTCOME OF THE DISCERNMENT PROCESS

Sometimes group members have strong desires for a particular outcome of a decision-making process. There is nothing wrong with hoping for a specific result, but it can be problematic if participants are not at the same time open to a variety of possible outcomes. Those who have a strong wish for their preferred outcome must resist the temptation to influence the group to move in that direction by lobbying for their point of view. Group members who favor a particular outcome must be self-aware and attentive to the Spirit. Being faithful to the process might be challenging, and they must come to each gathering resolved to listen intently and to question their own desires. The importance of coming to the prayer session with an open heart and mind becomes especially clear if several members of the group assume the same outcome or hope for the decision to go a certain way. Listening to the Spirit can be difficult if group members have already decided what will happen.

A discernment group was gathered to discern with Allison, who was considering a call to ordained ministry. Everybody wanted to be supportive of Allison and some of the group members even saw themselves serving primarily as advocates for Allison's admission to the church's ordination preparation process. A couple of members became concerned about this and how the process was progressing. They spoke up, urging Allison and the group to be sure to examine all the possible options and in doing so stay faithful to the discernment.

What Allison needed was a community to help her discern rather than a group of advocates. The advocates did not see themselves as pushing the group toward their desired outcome, truly believing they were doing discernment. They said they felt supporting Allison was very important because the ordination process was rigorous. The group was also experiencing pressure from the congregation to move Allison along in the ordination process. Allison's advocates in the discernment group were so convinced of their perspective that they were unable to listen to thoughtful questions or contrary opinions. Eventually, the group became contentious and split up. Allison was disappointed in the outcome and left the congregation. In the end, their effort to support Allison served neither her nor the purpose of the group.

BEING VULNERABLE

As group members gather together over time, they begin to reveal their most profound thoughts about self and God. This personal revelation contributes to a heart-felt intimacy among group members as they share some of their most private thoughts and feelings. When a group's trust level is high, members are willing to be vulnerable with each other, and relationships can grow ever deeper and more intimate. In the Prayer Model, a seeker may describe wrestling with spiritual doubts or difficult faith questions, and others may discover that they are wrestling with the same issues or questions. During the exploration component of the method, group members may learn that some of them have had similar life experiences. Taking the risk of allowing deeper intimacy with God, self, and the other is necessary for spiritual growth. Truly knowing God, ourselves, and others makes it possible to move from the known and static to exploring the unknown and changing. The Spiritual Discovery Method invites participants into these deeply personal and spiritually intimate relationships.

Participants may feel vulnerable as they enter into these intimate relationships and reveal some of their most personal struggles. Some may prefer to enter slowly into the process, frequently choosing to occupy the place of the compassionate observer. As they observe members serving as seeker or responder, they may gradually become more comfortable and willing to take on these speaking roles. A group member who is feeling vulnerable may choose the seeker role, discussing a topic that feels safe, thus allowing herself time to move to deeper subjects as she feels more comfortable. This gradual movement into vulnerability is especially appropriate if the person is new to the Prayer Model and discernment process.

Sometimes, however, a participant may be unable to overcome reluctance to join in such deep spiritual relationships. In such a case, this person may give herself permission to find an activity more suited to her comfort level. Another option would be for this member to always take the role of the compassionate observer, participating in the Prayer Model in silence before joining the discussion that follows. This option is recommended only if the group, for example, is a leadership council and desires that the member remain on the council.

As participants prepare for vulnerability in the Spiritual Discovery Method, they may find it helpful to think of prayer as the most intimate form of communication. Details that are never discussed with another person are brought to private conversation with God. Although these depths of intimacy may not be disclosed in a group, praying with others does provide an opening for developing intimate relationships. Participants always choose how much they will reveal about themselves, but as members of a group grow in trust, they are able to become increasingly self-revealing.

Silence in a group encourages intimacy. Silence does not often happen when people gather, as we tend to fill time with words. Relationships thrive and depend on verbal communication. Even though much communication is nonverbal and body language and facial expressions reveal a great deal about the words we speak, when words are removed from the situation, communication takes on a different quality. We might notice things about each other that we had not seen before—expressive eyes or subtle body language. Some nonverbal communication might happen intuitively, and we connect in a different way. Participants might describe this as seeing joy or pain or anger in someone's eyes, for example. This new kind of communication adds a deeper level of intimacy. The Spiritual Discovery Method, through corporate prayer and silence, encourages deeper intimacy among members of the group.

CHALLENGES WITH GROUP DYNAMICS

As in any gathering of people, group dynamics in discernment groups can be challenging. These dynamics have to do with the behavior of individual members, how others respond to that behavior, and the overall influence of the behavior on the group itself. Challenges may include such things as a member's tendency to monopolize the conversation, another's failure to contribute to the discussion, a participant who is always late, or someone who attends irregularly or unpredictably. Groups that function well will openly address these issues in a timely manner.

If a participant has stopped attending, for example, the group could designate a member to reach out to him, letting him know how his absence affects the group, and negotiate a resolution. The group members could discuss together the impact on the group of a participant's consistently late arrival, which interrupts the Prayer Model.

Each situation is unique and must be addressed as it arises. Hopefully, the group as a whole will respond to these difficulties. Sometimes, a group leader is required to gently and firmly respond to difficult situations. Group dynamics problems should not be ignored because they can eventually destroy a group. As participants address the challenges of group dynamics successfully, they will develop and reinforce skills, such as listening and speaking the truth in love, that contribute to positive group participation and shape stronger and closer groups.

Sometimes a consultant would be helpful for a group. For example, a group may find in the course of their work together that their discernment process becomes sidetracked because of some trouble with group dynamics. After doing what they can to work the problem themselves with no success, they may need to hire a consultant for a few meetings. A consultant brings a fresh, objective perspective of the situation along with skills that will be helpful to the group as they address their problem. The consultant would join the group only for as long as the group needs her assistance.

TIME PRESSURES

Groups engaging in spiritual discernment may experience challenges associated with the perception of time and how it is used. In order to forestall the very human drive in our busy world to produce tangible results and do it quickly, addressing these issues as they arise is essential. Succumbing to this drive inhibits the Spirit of God from doing its work. Such pressures can come from within the group, from outside the group, or both.

Time pressures from within the group can take many forms. Some members may be impatient and eager to finish the discernment. Others might begin to miss group meetings or their attention may begin to wander during meetings. When the group encounters what seems like a roadblock, instead of seeking to identify the underlying issue, one or two members might urge the group to move on past it and conclude the discernment.

A lack of understanding about the amount of time required for faithful spiritual discernment may create time pressures. Members may have joined the group without a clear agreement about how long the discernment would take and committed less time than was necessary for a faithful discernment process. In such a case, the group should revisit the subject or discuss it for the first time. They might also ask each other what would help relieve the time pressures some are feeling.

Time pressures may be imposed on the group from outside people who are eagerly anticipating a decision. They may not understand the nature of discernment and the time necessary for it to be completed. When the discernment group is listening and waiting, others may think the group is doing nothing. This then causes anxiety as they await a decision from the discernment group. Others may not think such a discernment process is necessary at all and view it as a waste of time.

Group members might respond to time pressures from outside the group by teaching about the discernment process. They are free to describe the operational details of the group's work, such as who is participating and how often they meet. They could talk about the importance of taking time to listen and wait for the Spirit. Group members, however, must avoid describing anything of the content of the group's discussions in order to maintain the necessary confidentiality of the discernment process.

Members of a discernment group know they are finished when they reach a general consensus that they have faithfully completed their discernment. Everyone concurs with the decision they have reached, though some may not agree with all that the decision implies. The group has a feeling of peace with the conclusion they have reached. Everyone agrees that they have been thorough and there is nothing more to pray about, explore, or discuss because they have created the opportunity for the Spirit of God to do its work and have been attentive in their listening.

GROUP MEMBERS "DISAPPEAR"

Sometimes members "disappear" from a discernment group. This might happen for several reasons: members move away, they take on other responsibilities, or the process takes longer than they expected, to name a few. Sometimes members disappear or stop attending because they don't think they can make a contribution. For example, members find that the decision-making process has a foregone conclusion and members cannot have a say. If one member seems to be driving the group in a particular direction, what others think doesn't seem to matter. No discernment is taking place. Membership in such a group can then become an unpleasant obligation. Unless these issues are addressed and members hold each other accountable, some may become disappointed with the process and drop out.

The leadership council of North Suburban Church of Christ was deciding if they should build a new sanctuary. One of the members of the council was the man who had proposed the idea and had already decided that the congregation needed the new building. He was somewhat forceful about it and had begun to promote his ideas in the congregation, gathering a small group of followers. In an effort to bring a prayerful approach to the decision and examine all the possibilities, the pastor formed a spiritual discernment group and asked them to advise the council about what they had discerned. The group consisted of a few members of the council, the pastor, the man whose idea was being considered, and several members from the congregation at large.

From the beginning, the man strongly advocated for his position. He was doing his best to influence the group to choose his "side" and often monopolized the exploration and discussion time. Group members became bored and disillusioned. Over the next few months, they began to make excuses and stopped attending the meetings. Eventually, only a few people were attending each meeting. Without enough participants, the group struggled to continue using the Prayer Model. Finally, over the objections of the man, the group agreed to stop meeting. The North Suburban leadership council would have to do its own discernment without the benefit of the Spiritual Discovery Method.

If members begin to drop out of a group, those who remain should examine the group dynamics, how the group was formed, and the essentials of the Spiritual Discovery Method. They will probably see some reasons that explain why they are missing group members. As in the group described above, where members were trying to influence the outcome and group dynamics became a problem, there may be obvious reasons why members have dropped out. Group members might also ask others who have left what drove them away. Although it can be challenging to address some issues, the answers will be well worth the effort.

LACK OF ACCOUNTABILITY

Another challenge to a successful experience with the method is lack of mutual accountability among the members of the group. All group members are responsible for how well the group functions. There are appropriate ways to hold each other accountable to the group's purpose and process.

If confidentiality is broken or a group member is trying to manipulate the outcome of a decision, others in the group—because they care for each other and desire the group to function as designed—will gently confront the unhealthy behavior. For example, if a participant begins to talk about the content of the prayer during the discussion time without asking the seeker's permission, respectfully reminding the participant that the content of the prayer must remain within the sacred container of the Prayer Model is appropriate. Doing so honors the seeker, the errant participant, and the entire group. It keeps the process safe for future seekers and prevents compromising the method. For the method to function at its best, group members should expect that, when necessary, they will be gently reminded of the group's norms. When the Spiritual Discovery Method is conducted faithfully, the exercise of mutual accountability is a valued part of the process.

THE DISCERNMENT PROCESS "FAILS"

Occasionally, the discernment process has been described as a failure. Following the completion of the group's work, someone may assess that the group has failed because they are dissatisfied with the decision that the group has made. Or the assessment of failure may take place during the life of the group when it encounters challenges that seem difficult to overcome.

If problems arise during the discernment process and group members think the process is failing, there could be a number of ways the causes of failure manifest themselves. For example, group members may express frustration with what feels to them like a lack of progress. They may begin to lose interest. A group may appear to be failing if members are attending but participating less and less in the discussion. The group may have become distracted by trivial concerns, such as administrative details, or members may not be able to move beyond surface issues because mutual trust has failed to develop.

At such a point, group members may ask themselves some questions. Did they clearly define the discernment question as they began their work together? Has the group been faithful in its practice of the Prayer Model at each meeting? Has confidentiality been broken so that trust is impaired? Is there an uncomfortable truth that remains unspoken and makes progress difficult? Have members called each other to account for their participation in the group? The group may need to explore many questions before they discover why their group doesn't seem to be working.

The group will benefit from a review of the design of the method and the essentials and challenges to identify reasons the process appears to be failing. Group members might also imagine what the process would look like if they were accomplishing their purpose. How might things be different? What could each person contribute toward a solution? The group should determine some clear and concrete steps they can take to get the group back on track. The group should continue to evaluate their progress and check in from time to time on how they are doing. With contributions from each member, perceived failure can lead to success, and the group will be strengthened by their commitment and hard work.

Sometimes members of a group will come to a decision, act on that decision, and then discover they have regrets about the decision. They may even think they made the wrong decision. Group members may experience this regret as a failure of the discernment process itself. A seeker, for example, may decide that he chose the wrong vocation. A pastor search committee may conclude that they made a serious mistake in their selection. A leadership group might decide on a course of action only to discover unexpected roadblocks in carrying out their plan. The Spiritual Discovery Method may lead to a result that not everyone considers right or desirable. The decision may not satisfy everyone involved in the process, or for that matter, *anyone* who participates or is affected.

Daniel was serving his congregation as member of the search committee, which was charged with calling a new senior pastor for their growing congregation. The group had narrowed the field to three candidates, all of whom were well qualified to lead the congregation into the future. As the group approached this final phase of their work, they continued faithfully to practice the Spiritual Discovery Method they had used to guide them through the decision-making process. Two candidates both had a strong following in the group, and the group was divided. Neither of the two factions wanted to back down, and discussions became more and more contentious. They seemed to be at an impasse, and some members stopped attending meetings, saying that the process had failed and it was a waste of their time.

Daniel saw things differently. He thought the group had done good work and resisted the conclusion that the process had failed. He asked the group to come back together and consider a third candidate. After a few weeks of prayer and discussion, the group eventually decided to call the third candidate. No one in the group was completely happy with the decision, but it seemed the only possible resolution. The new pastor was called. Over the succeeding years, many of the group members believed the "compromise" pastor was exactly what the congregation needed because they saw the congregation continuing to thrive. Time helped them to see that they had reached a successful decision.

When groups find themselves questioning the success of their decision, members may want to ask themselves some questions. What expectations were brought to the process? Did participants come to the group with assumptions about what would constitute success? Has enough time passed in order to truly assess the decision? Was the process a failure because the conclusion of discernment was not what was expected? Was it a failure if a group quit meeting before a decision was reached? How does one define success for the process?

Some participants might conclude the process has been a success if the result is that group members become better listeners. Success may be a surprise when, at the conclusion of discernment, the decision reached is not what was expected. Even if the group stops meeting before a decision is made, the group may have been successful in that the lives of members were changed in some way. Some might judge the process successful when group members are able to take some of the spiritual skills they learn out into the world. Others may define success as reaching a decision. Others may think of success as gaining a group of companions who have gathered to embark on a spiritual journey together.

Success may not be immediately recognizable. The effects of a decision may take months or years to be revealed. A seeker may take a long time to resolve a situation that had been shared with the group. A seeker might discover that success leads not to the resolution of a situation, but rather to acquiring better coping skills and peace with what cannot be changed. A seeker may reflect back on the gifts that were given by the group and how she has integrated them into her thinking. Since discernment is an ongoing process, the success of the method may indeed continue to be revealed over time. A seeker may even realize that what she once perceived as a failure of the discernment process, she later understands as a success.

Use of the Spiritual Discovery Method increases participants' awareness of the decision-making process, facilitates listening to the Spirit, and encourages clear and creative reflection. The method directs seekers in a process that helps them to discover their own deepest truth and to see how the Spirit is present in their lives. It provides groups with a way of coming together to explore the collective wisdom of its members. Overall, the Spiritual Discov-

ery Method creates a thoughtful and prayerful environment in which decisions can be made. The method is about the process of decision-making and
not about a predetermined result.

Participants may find themselves surprised by decisions they have
reached through the Spiritual Discovery Method. These outcomes may be
delightful or disappointing. They may appear contradictory. Outcomes might
be messy and even conflict with earlier decisions. Sometimes a decision must
be tested over time. But as long as participants have entered faithfully into
the discernment process with open hearts and minds, the process can be
trusted. It can be trusted to provide a setting in which the Spirit may speak. It
can be trusted to provide an opportunity to listen and hear the Spirit's voice.
The method creates an opening for the Spirit to act. Conclusions may be
messy, contradictory, or surprising *because* the method makes room for participants to hear the Spirit's voice. The Spirit does not promise neat and tidy
outcomes.

TAKING THE SPIRITUAL DISCOVERY METHOD INTO THE WORLD

In the discussion of the Prayer Model in part 1, we described some ways the
spiritual skills learned in the practice of the Prayer Model can be taken into
the world. So, too, spiritual skills developed during the practice of the Spiritual Discovery Method can be useful in the wider world. Some of these skills
have to do with the personal transformation of the individual who has participated in the method. These new skills change how individuals relate to the
world. Others are skills that a participant applies in the world by helping
other individuals and groups achieve fulfilling spiritual discernment in their
own lives. A spiritual discernment group as a whole can also become more
skilled as it practices the method and makes those group skills useful in the
world. Like a well-disciplined team, groups can work together effectively,
practicing their listening, discernment, and relationship skills in the service
of their congregations.

Spiritual skills are grounded in one's relationship with the Spirit of God.
For example, as a person experiences the love of God, he in turn learns to
love. As a person learns to trust God, that person begins to understand how
trust works in relationships. As one learns to value honesty and truth, she
learns how to live out those values in her relationships. A person's relationship with the Spirit of God shapes her relationships with others. The depth

and maturity of one's relationship with God is reflected in human relationships. A person who is wishing to develop her spiritual skills must begin by growing in her relationship with the Spirit of God while at the same time focusing on the skill she wishes to develop.

Participants learn to be present in relationships and conversations in new ways. For example, one who is generally extroverted can practice speaking less. The extrovert may wish to be present in a conversation as a compassionate observer, practicing both interior and verbal silence. He can be more reflective and attend to how the Spirit speaks within, and work at sharing thoughts that are more complete and focused. Or an introvert might realize that her thoughts are a work in progress. She might try to be more spontaneous as she speaks about how the Spirit is working within her. She learns that even these incomplete thoughts can contribute to the work of the group as they discern God's presence in the moment.

The group exploration and discussion portion of the Spiritual Discovery Method is a safe place for participants to test their spiritual learnings and practice new ways of engaging others. Because the group members have been growing in relationship with each other during the practice of the prayer, relational dynamics such as trusting and withholding judgment are present to some degree. For example, participants may come to the discussion more open and willing to be vulnerable, thus able to reveal their confusion and questions. They can learn to appreciate confusion and questions rather than needing to provide answers to dilemmas. They become more attentive listeners. They understand the presence of the Spirit. The process creates a place where participants can be more vulnerable and open with each other and with the Spirit.

The group's practice of the Spiritual Discovery Method creates opportunities to learn new spiritual skills, which can be taken into daily life outside the group. When we risk trying a new behavior with a group of people we trust and have a successful experiment, we are ready to try that new behavior in a larger arena. For example, Joe, the seeker who came to the discernment process to explore joining the governing council at St. John's, discerned that he was not called to serve on the board but rather to continue in his buildings and grounds ministry. He was able to say "no" to that particular invitation to service and choose what he thought God was calling him to do. In this new discernment process, Joe was able to listen to how the Spirit was speaking to him, was open to various possibilities, and was able to trust his colleagues to discern with him. These were all things that Joe learned from his experience of the discernment process. If someone in the community asked him to organize a community event, he could draw upon his participation in the discernment group and prayerfully discern how to respond. His experience of listening to the Spirit, being open, and trusting his companions serves him well in many different situations. Even without a group of companions to sit with him in prayer for each situation, the spiritual skills developed in the method overflow into everyday life.

Claudia was a member of a discernment group in her congregation. Through the use of the Spiritual Discovery Method, one of the skills the group had developed particularly well was encouraging all members to fully participate in the group by offering their wisdom. They all understood that the Spirit offered valued gifts through each member. They successfully managed the group discussion in a way that enabled everyone to participate. At first, one woman in the group had been very quiet. When other group members noticed this, they made sure that she was invited to speak up. The group quickly discovered the wisdom that this woman had to offer and deeply valued her contributions. Another member of the group tended to talk much more than others and sometimes monopolized the conversation. Others were able to gently help her to see how her behavior was preventing others from contributing. Eventually, the talkative woman was able to chuckle at herself when she caught herself "rambling on." The group members often reminded themselves that their efforts to hear from each member had helped the group work effectively.

When Claudia was asked to be on the Efficiency Task Force at the plant where she worked, she experienced some of the same dynamics in the task force's discussions. Her practice in the discernment group provided her with the skills and awareness she needed to see that a couple of task force members whose areas of expertise were essential to their work had been shut out of the discussions by another member who dominated the group. Claudia was able to ask questions of the quieter members and have their insights included in the discussion. She also found herself comfortable with being assertive enough to privately and compassionately approach the dominant member about how his behavior was affecting the group. Claudia's gentle but firm approach helped the man to see that he needed to work on getting his point across without dominating the conversation. The task force became a very effective group and was successful in its work. Although Claudia felt she was taking a risk by speaking the truth in love, she was glad that she had spoken up and had been able to help the group work together in a more positive and efficient way.

The Spiritual Discovery Method provides a structure in which group skills can be learned and practiced, and then taken into other settings. For example, as participants work to achieve positive group dynamics in their discernment groups, they can become more effective members in other groups. When individuals learn to keep each other accountable for their behavior in the discernment group, they can effectively use this skill in other groups. One who has participated in a group that has successfully defined its purpose and goals will be able to help another group do the same. These and other skills such as effective time management, keeping confidentiality, and being appropriately vulnerable are useful in any group. They are critical to the spiritual life of the group because they make it possible for participants to be attentive to the movement of the Spirit rather than being distracted by troublesome group dynamics.

Group members encourage each other in their spiritual growth. Their experience of supporting each other can be useful in relationships outside the group. When participants have used the method to examine their own spiritual questions and learned new skills in the process, they have begun to gain insights into themselves and how they might be called to grow and change. That development may be encouraged and supported by others in the group, even after the group completes its work. The intimacy and strong relationships that many group members have described become an ongoing influence in their lives, even after the group stops meeting. Group members have reported that they continue to have insights into their own spiritual dilemmas and life situations many months after their group has completed its work. Strong relationships and mutual support among group members endures. Although the spiritual journey is profoundly unique to each person, it takes place in community as well as in solitude. Group participants can be positive members of that larger community, having practiced how to be supportive and encouraging to others.

The ability to discern the Spirit's voice is valuable in any decision-making process. As groups and individuals make decisions using the Spiritual Discovery Method, they practice spiritual skills and habits that they can use to reach a decision even when the method is not used. For example, as group members practice silence and listening in the method, they can use their skills at remaining silent to listen deeply in any situation. Many decisions do not allow for group discernment. Some take months to make. Some situa-

tions require immediate decisions. A group or individual who has had practice making decisions using the method can trust the skills they have learned
and be more confident about their ability to make wise decisions in any
situation.

Groups and members of groups who have practiced spiritual skills can
become leaven in congregations and other institutions. Others who observe
their spiritual growth are drawn toward them. A healthy spiritual person or
group is attractive and draws others. A congregation can develop a core of
people who are growing spiritually, and others will recognize the congregation as a place where people can come to deepen their relationships and
experience personal and spiritual growth. The congregation is transformed
from within. A spiritual discernment group in the congregation can be an
essential part of the adult formation and prayer life of a congregation. Just as
the model and method are transformative for individuals, they are transformative for groups, congregations, and institutions.

The Spiritual Discovery Method provides a structure in which companions may shape how they journey together. Forming a community of prayer
whose members come together to listen to each other and the Spirit creates a
formative influence in the lives of its participants. This companionship is
inspiring as members encourage and challenge each other on the road. Having companions on the way helps participants discern the voice of the Spirit,
providing each one with more "ears" for hearing. Companions on the journey
enable each other to see things about themselves they might not see otherwise, helping each other grow in self-awareness. Sometimes hearing things
that are difficult or challenging is important. What better setting is there than
a group that prays together and speaks and listens within that prayer?

Group members have seen that truth is essential for effective discernment
and have found that healthy group life is helpful to a good decision-making
process. When one member of the group grows, all benefit. The collective
wisdom of the group becomes an asset to each member. As trust grows
among group members, mutual respect and care tend to grow as well. Participants may discover that their community has become very close and loving.
This group has experienced all the best that the Spiritual Discovery Method
offers.

Groups such as these eventually find that the members are consistently
"speaking the truth in love." Because what is spoken is immersed in prayer
and listening to each other and to the Spirit, it is both spoken and heard in a
context of compassion. For participants, being in the role of compassionate

observer may be the most powerful place in which one hears and experiences that compassionate word. In our next part, we will examine that role.

III

The Compassionate Observer

The role of the compassionate observer is both challenging and rewarding. It may appear that the silent compassionate observer is not substantially contributing to the process. However, as we reflect more fully on this role, we will see the profound contribution the compassionate observer brings to the Spiritual Discovery Method.

Chapter Thirteen

The Power of Compassion and Observation

The compassionate observer contributes to the process of group spiritual discernment by his presence and attention to the participants, the prayer, and the Spirit of God. He is a companion, a witness, and a host to the Spirit, who brings transformation. The compassionate observer strives for a keen sense of observation. As we shall see, these observational skills lead to heightened compassion. Such a compassionate observer finds himself changed by his practice of compassionate observation.

Jane Vennard characterizes the compassionate observer in a couple of different ways. In the first, she describes a triad in which the seeker, responder, and compassionate observer each attend to the others and to the Spirit in accord with the requirement of the roles. The seeker and responder speak and listen to one another. The compassionate observer is present and attends to the exchange. The compassionate observer, by his presence of compassion, helps to open the way for the Spirit of God.

The compassionate observer can be an instrument of the transformative power of the Spirit. In her book *Fully Awake and Truly Alive*, Jane Vennard provides insight into the contribution of the compassionate observer.

> I believe that showing up and seeing and feeling the situation with our minds and hearts, our very presence can open the way for the power of holy love and mercy to affect the situation. Through our witness, divine energy has the power to transform hearts and lives. Sometimes doing nothing lovingly allows something to happen. [1]

In the Spiritual Discernment Method, the compassionate observer, by "showing up" for the seeker and responders, provides companionship for the discernment process. When the compassionate observer is present, the seekers and responders are not alone, but are accompanied by someone whose sole responsibility is to listen and to pray. He is indeed a silent participant in the process, but, in doing so, he is a companion to the seeker, the responders, and the other compassionate observers.

This companionship is like what one might experience when she is asked to accompany a friend to a doctor's appointment. This companion shows up, bringing encouragement to her friend, who may be feeling vulnerable. The companion can sympathize and support the patient, helping to relieve anxiety the patient might be experiencing. In accompanying her friend to the doctor, the companion also serves as a witness. The companion listens carefully, noting questions from the patient and instructions from the doctor. The companion can verify what is said and, in doing so, shares the reality of the patient's experience. The patient and the doctor, in the presence of a witness, also behave differently than the way they would without the witness. They may be more attentive to what they say and how carefully they listen to each other. If the patient is calmed by the presence of her companion, she may think more clearly. Because of the presence of an observer, what happens between doctor and patient is changed. The role of the compassionate observer invites transformation.

Similarly, the compassionate observer shows up for the seeker and responders in the Spiritual Discernment Method. Through companioning and witnessing, the compassionate observer becomes a way for the power of holy love to enter into a situation. She creates a sacred space, inviting the divine energy that has the power to transform. As participants sit within the circle of compassionate observers in the Prayer Model, they are surrounded by love. The safety of the container that the compassionate observers create allows the seeker and responders to speak and listen freely, trusting that what they say will be held in compassion. As they pray, the compassionate observers say and do "nothing" lovingly, thereby allowing something to happen.

The role of the compassionate observer involves two different but related activities: observation and compassion. Each of these components has an impact on seekers and responders in the Prayer Model and is also influential in the discussion and exploration time.

The component of observation is described in a unique way by Quaker Thomas Kelly in his book *A Testament of Devotion*. He says that observation

is intensified when we involve all of our senses, including the full engagement of our spiritual awareness. Kelly calls this way of observing *hyperaesthesiac* (hyperaesthesia is the opposite of anesthesia).[2] Hyperaesthesiac observation requires all of our capacity to take in what is around us with our
senses, intuition, and spirit. This kind of observation makes it possible to
experience the beauty and the brokenness around us with profound intensity.
The hyperaesthesiac observer senses himself, others, and all of creation with
a new clarity, depth, and truth.

Where he didn't see before, such an observer now sees deeply. Kelly also
says that for this observer, "Creation has a new smell."[3] Things around him
may be the same, but somehow, his relationship with creation changes as he
experiences it hyperaesthesiacally. Kelly says that in this experience, the
observer's soul is "tendered,"[4] and he is now wholly aware of things that he
had not sensed before. Not only does he perceive with new eyes and ears, but
he sees and hears with spiritual eyes and ears. This kind of observation opens
him to the power of compassion. The tendered soul senses the presence of the
Holy in all things and is compelled to compassion.

For the compassionate observer, compassion shapes observation. A compassionate observer witnesses with a heart of love. She simply holds what
she sees in love and compassion. The observer sees the seeker and loves. She
hears his dilemma with compassion, "feeling with" the seeker. She fills the
silence with love. She also observes the responders lovingly, grateful for the
gifts they offer the seeker. Her desire is to see as the Spirit of God sees—with
a heart filled with love.

In the Prayer Model, the seeker's experience of compassionate observation transforms the practice of seeking. A seeker held in a circle of compassion knows that she is held in love. That circle creates a safe container, and
the seeker knows that what she says will be heard with compassion. The
seeker also knows that the compassionate observers are attending to the
presence of the Spirit and are inviting her to listen to what the Spirit is saying
to her. Her seeking is changed by the healing and creative presence of the
Spirit.

In addition to receiving the love of the compassionate observers, a seeker
may come to the Prayer Model seeing her own dilemma differently because
she has already filled the role of compassionate observer. She has practiced
seeing with compassion and is more able to see herself and her situation with
compassion, which changes what she seeks. For example, a seeker who in the
past struggled to be forgiving now sees herself with compassion and under-

stands that forgiveness is a complex process and takes time. She sets realistic expectations for herself and enters into her dilemma holding herself gently as she works through a process of forgiving herself. Her process of seeking is changed because she has learned to be a compassionate observer for herself.

The experience of being a compassionate observer can also change how one responds. The responder understands that the source of his response to the seeker is the Spirit of God, rather than his own ego. His intention is to make way for the Spirit to act, thereby "allowing" something to happen, rather than making it happen. He no longer needs to do or say anything with the goal of changing the seeker, because he has seen the result of showing up with compassion in his heart. He is able to relinquish the desire to fix or advise. Such a responder also knows the circle to be a safe and loving place to speak. As he listens to the Spirit, he is supported by his companions, who are listening with him and holding him in love. His desire is that his words are the words of the Spirit speaking through him.

In addition to benefitting the seeker and responders, the practice of compassionate observation has advantages for the compassionate observer herself. As she listens intently to others, she finds herself developing a deeper compassion for the seeker and responders, and also for herself. Her perception and understanding of others helps her to know herself more honestly and lovingly.

Compassionate observation is also beneficial during the discussion and exploration time. For example, any participant may decide to take some time out to be silent and observe the conversation with compassion. This gives her an opportunity to look deeply into a situation and notice things she may not have heard before. Her keen observation gives her a new perspective. She may hold others in compassion and listen to the Spirit. When she chooses to rejoin the conversation, she has a deeper understanding and greater compassion. The quality of her participation has changed.

Another example of how the compassionate observer can be helpful during a group's discussion time is for the group to ask one or more of its members to act as a compassionate observer while the rest of the group enters into conversation. Such a compassionate observer may be physically present at the gathering or serve at a distance during the deliberations. These groups find their conversation transformed as a result of the presence of the compassionate observers. They have become aware that they occupy a sacred space and that their conversation is held in prayer.

Chapter Fourteen

The Disciplines of the Compassionate Observer

The disciplines of compassionate observation assist the observer in being fully attentive to the prayer, its participants, and the presence of the Spirit. While the primary responsibility of the compassionate observer is to serve the group and the spiritual discernment process, the disciplines of quietness and concentration may also be beneficial to the compassionate observer herself.

BEING QUIET

The most distinctive discipline of the compassionate observer is that of being quiet. Because the compassionate observer does not speak during the Prayer Model, she has the opportunity to pay close attention not only to remaining silent, but also to quieting herself in body, mind, and spirit. Her peacefulness also reduces distractions for all of the participants.

During the prayer, compassionate observers may begin by sitting in a relaxed, comfortable posture. Deep and steady breathing helps the body to relax. Some compassionate observers prefer to keep their eyes closed throughout the prayer, while others would rather look at the inner circle of speakers. As the body rests, the compassionate observer may begin to notice areas of physical stress or discomfort and focus on releasing them. A practice that may be useful is letting go of tension in one part of the body and allowing that feeling to move through the body until she is relaxed and peaceful.

Once physical distractions are relinquished, the compassionate observer is free to notice her state of mind. Quieting the mind presents its own particular challenge. In the midst of silence, the mind may become full of thoughts and emotions. These can become such a distraction that the compassionate observer is no longer able to be present to the prayer. She may address the distraction by gently returning to the prayer as soon as she notices that her mind is wandering. She may choose a short mantra or sacred word and repeat it silently to herself. At first, this cycle of distraction and attention may occur frequently, but over time and with practice, the mental distractions will decrease. She must be patient with herself as she perseveres in returning to the prayer. There is no need for self-blaming here, just determination and trust in her ability to succeed in quieting her mind.

Once the mind is quiet, the compassionate observer is able to go deeper and allow her inner spirit to become quiet. This quieting is not a matter of doing something but a quality of being. The human spirit is intimately grounded in the Spirit of God, and a compassionate observer who is quiet and focused is better able to be open and receptive to that Spirit of God. All participants benefit when compassionate observers bring this quiet spirit, creating a tranquil and peaceful container upon which the entire group can depend.

All these disciplines of quiet are useful not only to the prayer but also to the compassionate observer. Letting go of the distractions of body, mind, and spirit and being quiet help the compassionate observer be attentive to all of life. She can be present in every moment, and by doing nothing, allow something to happen. Practices such as those described above and many others can lead to a deep state of quiet, freeing the Spirit within us. They help us to listen and connect to the Spirit within.

BEING CONCENTRATED

As an adult student of piano, I (Catherine) was playing through a Beethoven sonata for my teacher. I had successfully played it many times, but this time I had trouble getting through a particular passage. My teacher asked me why, and I told him I was having trouble concentrating. He replied, "Don't concentrate, *be* concentrated!"

As I later reflected on this, I realized that I no longer needed to struggle to concentrate or wrestle with distractions. Instead, I could choose to become concentrated. Being concentrated was not something I had to *do*. I was freed from trying to accomplish something and instead could decide what I was going to be. It was no longer about struggling to concentrate, but of knowing every detail and nuance of the music—infinitely deep and fascinating and beautiful—and about knowing it so thoroughly that it became a part of me. In this process, I found myself so thoroughly in the embrace of the music that distraction seemed irrelevant and indeed impossible.

Our doing flows out of our being. It becomes a manifestation of our being. We constantly make choices about who we are, and we can choose to be concentrated, to be compassion, to be peace, or even to be prayer. The apostle Paul makes this point when he appeals to the Thessalonians to pray without ceasing. For him, one's life must be prayer. Paul is pleading: Don't pray, *be* prayer! (1 Thessalonians 5:17)

Chapter Fifteen

Challenges for the Compassionate Observer

Being distracted is a common experience for the compassionate observer. She may be pondering the day's events or checking her mental "to do" list. Her own life issues may be capturing her thoughts. She may be worried or distracted by world events. Something in the physical environment, such as noise or the temperature of the room, can disrupt her focus. The seeker's presentation may resonate with the compassionate observer's own experience, and as a result, she loses herself in her own thoughts and feelings. The compassionate observer can become preoccupied with the seeker's dilemma or curious about details that are missing from the seeker's presentation. She is advised to let go of these distractions and refocus on her role, allowing the distractions to fall away. By refocusing, she can resolve to renew her compassion for the seeker and responders and move more deeply into prayer. A new compassionate observer may need to do this a number of times during the prayer, but over time, the distractions appear less frequently and are dismissed more easily.

The compassionate observer may have a strong desire to "fix" or advise the seeker. Resisting the desire to fix or advise may be especially difficult if she has had an experience similar to what the seeker is presenting. She might become convinced that how she handled her experience or the solution that she came to will be just what the seeker needs to hear. She may feel certain the Spirit has provided her with a critical insight for the seeker's benefit, and she finds it very difficult to remain silent and focused. In this event, the compassionate observer needs to remain faithful to her crucial role of compassionate observation, rejecting the temptation to step into the role of responder. She must remind herself to trust that if the insight is needed, the Spirit will provide some way for the seeker to receive it.

If a seeker expresses intense feelings—especially painful ones—during her presentation, a compassionate observer may become uncomfortable. This challenge requires the compassionate observer to return her focus to the seeker and let go of her own discomfort. She can deeply empathize and renew her compassion for the seeker. If the compassionate observer can forget herself in that moment, the discomfort will dissolve. Once again, the compassionate observer will be most effective if she can continually recommit herself to her role.

Judgment may be the most difficult challenge for the compassionate observer. To judge is to come to or hold an opinion about something. Judgment itself is a neutral thing. However, sometimes a particular judgment is fair, reasonable, and compassionate, and sometimes it isn't. It can be harsh or negative, especially when we judge each other. We might be judged by family members, teachers, employers, friends, and strangers. We can judge with little thought, and our judgments can be painful for those we judge, leaving a residue of shame on them. We often have difficulty *not* judging. When we are judged, we more easily dwell on a negative judgment than accept a positive one. A judgment can be difficult to change and impossible to forget.

We are often our own most critical judge and may have difficulty not judging ourselves. Sometimes, our self-judgment can be a result of or lead to holding ourselves to impossibly high standards. If we hold ourselves to high standards, we might feel virtuous, but our scrupulosity can become a source of pride. Likewise, we might hold others to the same unrealistic standards we hold for ourselves, and we then find ourselves making judgments about others as well. This judgment inhibits compassion for ourselves and others. If we habitually choose judgment, we rule out compassion.

If we can let go of judgment, we will change how we see ourselves and others. As we begin to recognize our judging when we are compassionate observers in the Prayer Model, we also become more aware of our judging in other situations. In that awareness, we can choose not to judge but rather to see with compassion. We can make this choice of compassion both for ourselves and for others.

SEEING WITH EYES OF COMPASSION

Imagine you are in a poorly lit room. If you are there long enough, you might become accustomed to the dim light and adjust your behavior to accommodate it. For example, you might move about carefully, feeling your way around the room until you learn where everything is without having to see it. You might not bother to decorate with visual art, since it would be hard to see and appreciate. You may not dust as often, because you cannot see the dirt. Then one day, you bring in a new lamp. When you turn it on, you are shocked at what you see. The walls of the room are dingy and need painting. Dust and dirt cover the furniture and floor. You find that button that fell off your sweater a while ago. Without any artwork, the room is drab and ugly. The room had been comfortable before, but now you don't want to sit in the stained chair or breathe the dusty air. The light from the new lamp seems harsh and painfully revealing. What it reveals, although perhaps you should not have been surprised, makes you embarrassed about how messy you let the room become. Now you have a choice. You can take away the new lamp, remain in the shadows, and forget about what it revealed, or you can clean up the mess and decorate the room.

Abundant light came into the room and brought knowledge. The knowledge was painful. The light did not judge, but by its nature, it revealed what was in the shadows. Your laziness or ignorance is now seen. Nothing is hidden. You might feel judged or indicted, but that is your feeling, not what the light did. Perhaps we characterize God as a judge because we feel judged when the light of the Spirit comes into our hearts. But the Spirit of God *is* light—the light that has come into the world and enlightens all things. When the light comes into our lives, we begin to see in ways we have not seen before.

In part 2, we describe spiritual discernment as seeing with spiritual eyes, from God's vantage point. The vantage point of the God is one of love (I John 4:8). Because God loves us first, we learn how to love and what being loved means. We begin to know what loving ourselves and others means. Our love is rooted in God's love. Our compassion is also rooted in God's compassion. As we are observed with compassion, we learn to be compassionate, because God is compassionate with us first. Because God sees us with eyes of compassion, we are able to see with eyes of compassion. When we see with eyes of compassion, judgment falls away. We learn love and compassion when we see from God's vantage point.

God does not judge. God enlightens. God loves. Because we have been loved and have been observed by God with compassion, we also love and observe ourselves and others with compassion.

THE COMPASSIONATE OBSERVER EXERCISE

Letting go of judgment and choosing compassion for ourselves and others is a discipline and requires practice. We can practice being our own compassionate observer by using the Compassionate Observer Exercise. This is a meditation that can be done in groups or by individuals for themselves.

Participants stand, if they are able. Each participant should allow sufficient space for two people to stand facing each other. Because participants do the exercise with their eyes closed, they might want to have something to hold on to, such as the back of a chair. If a participant is not able to stand, she may place two chairs facing each other and sit in one of them, leaving the other unoccupied. One person verbally guides the rest through the exercise.

Participants are instructed to begin by closing their eyes and taking a few deep breaths. The guide asks the participants to pay attention to their bodies, focusing on possible places of tension, pain, or stress. She asks whether they are feeling fatigued or rested, peaceful or strong? Participants take a minute for this interior examination.

Next, participants are guided to take note of their thoughts and emotions. Do they have a sense of well-being, feel centered, find focusing easy? Or are their thoughts racing, scattered, or wandering? Do they feel anxious or angry, or are they at peace or joyful? Is their spirit uneasy or settled, present and peaceful or distracted and disturbed? Is their spirit wrestling with something?

After participants have taken some time to notice their bodies, minds, emotions, and spirits, the guide directs them to physically turn around (or move to the other chair) and, with eyes still closed, face the opposite direction. They then "look" at themselves, at all of themselves: bodies, minds, emotions, and spirits.

What happens when the participant observes herself? She may notice negative thoughts or feelings of judgment, thoughts that elicit shame, embarrassment, or feelings of inadequacy. If so, the guide invites her to physically take a step to the side and see herself from another angle, letting go of the judgment and looking at herself with compassion. After a few moments of observing herself from the new angle, the participant is guided to take note of any feelings of judgment or negativity that arise. If needed, she should step to the side again, let go of the feelings of judgment, and see herself with compassion. The participant might need to view herself from several new angles before she begins to be filled with compassion for herself and is able let go of judgment and negativity.

The Compassionate Observer Exercise provides a participant the experience of choosing compassion rather than judgment. The exercise is a reminder of how easy it is to unconsciously fall into negativity and judgment when observing oneself. It helps counteract the tendency to judge oneself and encourages a participant to see herself with compassion. One thing that may become clear as she learns to be a compassionate observer is that she can *choose* compassion over judgment or negativity.

Nonjudgmental perception is a skill and can be developed. It needs to be practiced like other spiritual skills learned in the Spiritual Discernment Method such as listening, seeking, and self-awareness. Whenever the compassionate observer begins to notice judgment creeping into his perception, he can let go of it and begin to observe with compassion. If the judgment re-emerges, again he lets it fall away. Judgment is perceived and then intentionally released. Compassion is renewed.

As we observed in our discussion of the Vennard Prayer Model, the role of the compassionate observer is learned and understood through practice, experience, and reflection. A participant *becomes* a compassionate observer by taking on the role in the Spiritual Discernment Method, doing the compassionate observer exercise and practicing compassionate observation in life situations. Being a compassionate observer is learned by experience, not grasped by the intellect alone. After much practice, the compassionate observer begins to say to herself, "Ah, now I see."

TAKING THE COMPASSIONATE OBSERVER INTO THE WORLD

Being a compassionate observer in the world is much the same as serving as a compassionate observer in the Prayer Model. As we encounter others and engage in the activities of everyday life, there are times when it is best to remain silent and merely to compassionately observe. In such circumstances, we are given the opportunity to listen, create sacred space, and welcome the Spirit of God into the situation. In doing so, we view the situation or person from God's perspective, offering love and compassion as we observe.

Carol relied on compassionate observation through a difficult time in her life. She had an elderly aunt who lived close by. Because Carol was her aunt's only relative in town, she felt obligated to visit regularly and did so every week. Aunt Celeste was a complainer, finding fault with the caretakers who brought her meals and gave her medications. She even complained about Carol, accusing her of not caring and being selfish. Carol found the visits exhausting and depressing, but she also felt guilty about not doing more for Aunt Celeste.

Carol sought the support of her spiritual discernment group that had been meeting for years. They had regularly practiced the Spiritual Discovery Method, which gave Carol many opportunities to be a compassionate observer. The group had also regularly done the compassionate observer exercise. Through the years, Carol thought she was beginning to understand the compassionate observer. She found that she was able to be a compassionate observer for herself as she became less judgmental and more forgiving of her own foibles and faults. She described herself as "gentler companion," free to be truthful without shaming and to love without reservation.

As Carol grew in her practice of being a compassionate observer for herself, she noticed that she was also able to be a compassionate observer with others, and especially with Aunt Celeste. Although she was distracted by her judgment of others from time to time, her awareness of those judgments grew, and she found she more easily let go of them. She also noticed that she became comfortable with silence and was more focused as she listened. When it seemed important, she could be quiet and wait for others to speak.

When Aunt Celeste was dying, Carol sat with her in comfortable silence or listened when she wanted to talk. Sometimes Carol just sat and held her aunt's hand. The two of them became companions during the last weeks of Aunt Celeste's life, talking about spiritual things and laughing together as they remembered family stories. Before she died, Aunt Celeste, even though she remained a complainer to the end, told Carol how important her loving and quiet presence was to her. Aunt Celeste said that Carol's presence had helped to her to be more aware of how God was present in this holy dying time. She said she knew she could be difficult at times and was thankful for Carol's patience and forgiveness. Aunt Celeste thanked Carol for being a devoted niece and gave her a treasured family heirloom as a reminder of the time they had shared. As a result of their time together, Carol knew her aunt more intimately than she ever had before. In the end, Carol was deeply grateful for Aunt Celeste, even though the relationship had sometimes been difficult.

In Carol's story, both Carol and Aunt Celeste changed. Carol could see that her choice to be a compassionate observer for Aunt Celeste had helped them to grow closer and share a sacred time together. In other situations, the compassionate observer may never know whether or how her presence has made a difference. The compassionate observer creates a sacred space for the Spirit and entrusts the rest to God. This may happen in a grocery store when a compassionate observer is present to an angry exchange between a customer and a supervisor, when she encounters a "road rage" incident, or in any number of other everyday occurrences in the world.

I (Sandy) remember being on a cross-country overnight flight and watching as a woman across the aisle was apparently suffering from an asthma attack. The woman was being attended to by the flight crew and a physician. I noticed that the woman appeared to be part of a large group, and its members were very distressed by their friend's critical plight. I held the woman, the medical attenders, and the woman's friends in prayer throughout the incident and until the plane landed. I never said anything to anyone about it, nor did I learn how the incident was eventually resolved. I just did what I could to create a sacred space and trusted the rest to God.

The compassionate observer is present to the world in a way that is open to the Spirit of God. He is present, seeing and feeling what happens. He may not seem to be doing anything, but is holding a space for compassion and witnessing with love in his heart. He is creating a space in which those he encounters can take notice of the presence of the Spirit. This offering makes room for possibility. Where there is possibility, a seed of hope is planted, and new life begins to grow.

IV

Applying the Method

The cases of St. John's and Christ Church are two examples of how the
Spiritual Discovery Method has been used in congregations. Both of these
congregations look back on their experience of the method with a sense of
gratitude and appreciation as they continue to see the positive effects of the
prayer and discernment on their leadership groups and congregations.

At St. John's, this can be seen in the way the leadership group continues
to approach its work. Each year, the council and prospective members use
the method to discern who is called to join the group. Every meeting begins
with a check-in time, followed by a sharing of concerns and thanksgivings as
they pray together. The council folds other elements of the method into their
meetings by including moments of silence, prayerful listening, and employ-
ing compassionate observers to hold them in prayer. Following a stewardship
campaign where they used the method for planning, they noticed a deeper
and more positive commitment to the campaign than in previous years. Congregation members grew in their ability to listen respectfully, consider differing points of view, and discern the presence of the Spirit as they engaged in a
variety of activities. The pastor of St. John's observed that this was the wisest
and most thoughtful council he had worked with in the twenty years he had
served the congregation.

At Christ Church, the board of trustees reported that their use of the
method helped them to prayerfully take into account a number of factors
involved in the substantial project of planning for and bringing about their

merger. They invited consultation from members of the congregation who identified issues they had not previously considered. As they began to search for a potential partner congregation, they discussed geographical location, worship and architectural preferences, leadership styles, finances, pastoral care, ministry focus, demographics, and other factors. The leaders of Christ Church were very satisfied with their process and felt hopeful and encouraged about the possibilities for ministry in the merged congregation. The Christ Church board invited their new partners in ministry to practice the Spiritual Discovery Method with them and imagine ways they could continue its use together in the future.

Both St. John's and Christ Church leadership groups used the Spiritual Discovery Method diligently during their discernment. They faithfully followed the process using the Prayer Model at every meeting and brought the skills they learned into their discussions. After concluding their discernment, both groups continued to include components of the method in all their gatherings. They also found that they could make use of the method or components of the method in other groups. Some members reported they were successful in transferring skills they had learned into aspects of their personal lives. The fruit of the Spiritual Discovery Method continues to be manifest in these congregations in a number of ways.

When a congregational group uses the Spiritual Discovery Method, its application is usually intended for a specific discernment issue. For example, a congregational leadership council might be deciding about expanding the church staff, calling a new pastor, or remodeling the sanctuary. It may be that they want to revisit and update their vision and mission statements. They may decide to devote a retreat to their discernment.

In planning such a retreat, the leadership group must first be clear about the discernment question and secondly identify the crucial components involved in the question. The group may use the method as the meeting structure and choose a topic for each work session that addresses an aspect of their discernment question. A seeker brings his personal thoughts and feelings about the chosen topic or presents a story about how the issue in question touches his life. During the discussion, the group then addresses the predetermined topic and the larger discernment question. For example, a group deciding about expanding the church staff might use the first session to pray about and discuss the overall needs of the congregation. A second session could cover the financial resources available. A third might examine the overall staff structure and where the new person would fit within it. A final session could begin to create a job description. The participants will thus have had a chance to pray about and reflect carefully on a variety of aspects of the situation as they move toward a final decision.

A council might decide to use the Spiritual Discovery Method on a regular basis, at every third or fourth meeting for example. Or they might choose to use the method on an occasional basis as appropriate to the decisions before them at the time. In either case, the method will have a positive influence as members become comfortable with the use of the prayer, grow in the depth of their listening, and practice other skills encouraged by the use of the method.

Throughout this book, there are a number of stories about groups using the Spiritual Discovery Method. Many who have experienced the method in various circumstances have found it useful both for their groups and in their personal lives. In this part, we illustrate a number of additional ways the method can be adapted in congregational groups, by groups outside of congregations, and in secular settings.

A SERVICE OR OUTREACH GROUP

Although it may seem that the Spiritual Discernment Method would most appropriately apply to groups engaged in contemplative activities, it has also been effectively used by groups whose identity and focus are on active ministry in the world. One such group was made up of members of Prince of Peace Church who had signed up for a mission trip to help with earthquake recovery in Haiti. Ron was organizing the group, and they had ten months to prepare for the trip.

Ron and a couple of the Prince of Peace members had been a part of a group that used the Spiritual Discernment Method while engaged in a program of feeding the homeless. That group regularly used the method to help its volunteers reflect on their experiences with the homeless guests. Ron thought the method might be valuable for the Haiti mission group, so he suggested they use it as they conducted their planning and preparation meetings.

At their first gathering, Ron introduced the method to the group. He asked for volunteers to help demonstrate how it worked. Taking the place of the seeker, Ron asked another experienced group member to serve as timekeeper and had the volunteer responders and compassionate observers arrange themselves into their circles. Following the Prayer Model, the group debriefed their experience, took a break, and continued with exploration and discussion as outlined in the method. They concluded by deciding they would like to use the method regularly.

At their next meeting, a volunteer seeker shared something of her fears and uncertainties about the upcoming trip. She was concerned about how she might be affected by the need and suffering that she would witness in Haiti. As the group moved into its discussion, the seeker agreed to open the topic of her presentation for further exploration. Several said they felt relieved to know that they were not the only ones feeling anxious about the coming trip. They talked together about how they could courageously and compassionately go to a place where they would probably encounter experiences very different from anything they had ever known.

Each meeting began with a gathering time and the Prayer Model. A volunteer seeker presented a spiritual dilemma that developed for him as a result of the challenges facing the group as they prepared for their mission trip. As they shifted into the discussion, they were guided by the planning needs of their work, a text about the mission field, or a specific issue raised by their preparation. Each member had an opportunity to serve as the seeker prior to the group's departure for Haiti.

Over the months of preparation, the mission group brought issues to the prayer and, as permitted by the seeker, explored them during the discussion time. They reflected on topics such as feeling helpless in the midst of suffering, being overwhelmed by the devastation, and fearing the risks they might be taking. When the group gathered for their final planning meeting, members said they were grateful for their months of prayer and reflection and felt more prepared for the trip than for any other outreach work they had done in the past. One put it this way: "I definitely feel called to serve the people of Haiti and have no doubt that God will nurture the seeds we plant there. I also believe that God will nurture the seeds that are planted in my heart."

As a result of their experience during the planning, group members said they wanted to have time to prayerfully process their experiences during the trip itself, so they scheduled four gatherings while they were in Haiti. Participants were able to process their reactions to the many unanticipated aspects of their experience. They found that their prayer and reflection was a source of strength and encouragement in the midst of devastation that they witnessed.

The group continued using the method following their return home. When it came time for them to bring closure to their mission, members did several things. First, they offered thanksgivings for their Haiti experience, for the people they got to know there, and for their fellow travelers. They also acknowledged feeling very grateful for the opportunity they had had to explore the experience prayerfully. One said, "This trip was more fruitful for me in my spiritual life than any other experience I have ever had." Another commented that the prayerful approach to the trip had helped her to be more fully present to the grief and loss she observed among the victims of the earthquake. One of the group, who was a nurse, had worked in a makeshift camp hospital. She said her experience forever changed how she would practice nursing. The Spiritual Discovery Method helped group members see how prayer and action inform each other. Ron was thankful for the method and how it had enriched the experience for everyone, including himself.

YOUTH GROUP

Krista was the Youth Minister at her church where she had served for two years. During that time, she had gained the trust of the teens, so it was no surprise when a crisis at their high school brought them to her for support and comfort. One of their classmates had committed suicide, and although most of them had not been close friends with him, they were all distressed by what had happened. Krista heard them asking a number of questions, such as: "Could I have done something to prevent this?," "Is suicide a sin against God?," "What if I was thinking about suicide, too?," and "Where is God in all this?"

Listening to the teens, Krista realized that it might be helpful to find a way to take these questions into prayer. She had been a member of a discernment group that used the Spiritual Discovery Method and thought it might work for the teens in their pain and confusion. She prepared a handout summarizing the Spiritual Discovery Method and selected a curriculum on teen suicide and depression. At the next Youth Group meeting, she explained the method and asked the members if they would like to try it. Several of them were interested, so Krista set up a schedule of one meeting a month for the next few months to try the method with the students who wanted to participate. She asked for a volunteer to be the seeker at the first meeting.

As the meeting date approached, Krista prepared a room and gathered the necessary equipment. The small group of eight teens and Krista began with a refresher on how the method worked. They then prayed together and debriefed the prayer. The seeker said that she had been nervous at first, but she knew everyone in the group and was grateful that they were praying with and for her. One of the responders admitted, "I had no idea what I was going to say, but the Spirit spoke to my heart and I was moved to share that." Another said, "I thought the silence would be really uncomfortable, but it turned out to be powerful because it helped me be aware of the presence of God."

The group took a break and reconvened for the discussion. The young people talked openly with each other about their own experiences. They explored what they might do if someone they knew was talking about suicide or depression. They imagined how they might support each other and others who might be suffering. At the end of their discussion, they prayed for each other and the family of the teen who had died.

Over the next few months, the small group added a few members and continued praying using the Prayer Model and exploring the theme of suicide and depression. They found that the method helped them express their feelings and listen more carefully to each other. It brought them closer and helped them be more attentive to how those around them were doing. Several said they had gotten used to the silence and liked how it helped them focus. One student, who was going off to college the next year, talked about the possibility of starting a group with his peers and using the method to help them cope with situations they would encounter at the university. Another said the skills he learned from doing the method had made it possible for him to reflect on and discuss sensitive issues that he found were often difficult to address in other settings. Another teen said the method helped her to put words to what she was feeling which gave her courage to talk about her feelings with others. As they completed the suicide and depression program, Krista and the teens decided to continue using the Spiritual Discovery Method, especially when they thought it would help them deal with other challenging subjects.

ADULT EDUCATION GROUP

Anna was the adult education director at her church. Following each educational program she planned and implemented, she requested feedback from participants. From time to time, someone would express a hope for engaging in "something more," although what that meant was rather vague. Participants said they wanted to "dig deeper" or "wrestle with the big faith questions."

For her next adult education program, Anna proposed forming a "Something More" group. Its purpose would be to "dig deeper" and "wrestle with the big faith questions." Anna took seriously these expressions of longing for "something more," and as she was familiar with the Spiritual Discovery Method, she decided to introduce it to the "Something More" group and suggest that it be used for their meeting sessions. She recruited eleven people who agreed to commit to the group for a year. She asked them to prepare for their first meeting by reading about the Spiritual Discovery Method.

At that meeting, group members introduced themselves. They discussed what they had read about the method and, based on that reading, they made some decisions about how to proceed. They considered a number of books that would focus their discussion and exploration time—books about religion in contemporary culture, biographies, prayer methods, theological fiction, and spiritual classics. They selected a book about spiritual practices and chose the chapters they would read for their next meeting.

They discussed the structure for their future meetings. One person would serve as a seeker, bringing a story, dilemma, or a question to the Prayer Model. That seeker's focus might be on the book discussion topic or on another subject of his choice. They would take a break between the Prayer Model and the discussion time. If the seeker permitted, what had been shared during the Prayer Model could be discussed during the second half of the meeting. Otherwise, they would proceed with their discussion of the book they had read. Anna would create a brief ritual for the opening and for the closing of each meeting. They settled on group norms, which included agreements about confidentiality, attendance, refreshments, and the like. One member volunteered to be the seeker for their first experience with the Prayer Model.

At that meeting, they began with check-in, and after a review of the model and the roles, Anna led the group through the Prayer Model for the first time. The seeker presented an issue she had been wrestling with in her spiritual life. Following the prayer, they debriefed their experience, took a break, and then began the discussion and exploration. Their reading about spiritual practices sparked a discussion about how and why members might want to try new prayer techniques. Each participant committed to trying a new kind of prayer for the next month and report back to the group. The group agreed on their next reading assignment, and another member volunteered to be the seeker. They closed the meeting with a blessing ritual in which members stood in a circle, passed a candle around, and prayed silently for each person as she held the candle.

For the rest of the year, the group maintained a similar structure at their monthly meetings. Participants took turns filling the roles of the seeker, responder, and compassionate observer. The debriefing process revealed that group members were experiencing the roles more deeply and growing in their ability to discern how the Spirit was guiding them.

As the year came to a close, they agreed that they had certainly "gone deeper" and "wrestled with big spiritual questions." They decided to continue meeting and proceeded to regroup and re-contract with group members. One member decided to leave the group to start a Bible study group and was looking forward to incorporating the Spiritual Discovery Method into that group's work. Another was moving out of the area. For the last meeting that year, the group created a closing ritual, which included a farewell for the two members who were leaving. Then they planned how they would recruit and welcome two new members. They took the next month off and began again with their new membership. The "Something More" adult education group continued to meet for several more years.

BIBLE OR BOOK STUDY

As a member of the "Something More" adult education group, Bruce had found the experience deeply meaningful because of the way it helped him integrate spiritual discovery with learning. For some time, he had felt a need to undertake serious Bible study and was becoming aware that there were other folks with similar desires who might be interested in forming a Bible study group. It occurred to Bruce that the Spiritual Discovery Method might work well for such a group as it had for the book studies the "Something More" group had done together.

Bruce invited the interested people to join him and proposed they use the Spiritual Discovery Method as a structure for their Bible study. He suggested some books of the Bible that offered a rich opportunity for spiritual reflection, and together they selected one for their first venture. He then introduced them to the Spiritual Discovery Method, asked for a volunteer to serve as seeker, and set the date and time for their first meeting. The group met for many months thereafter and selected new books of the Bible for study from time to time, adapting the group's membership as they progressed. Over the years, the group has changed membership as people have left and joined. The Bible study group continues to meet to this day.

Groups that use the Spiritual Discovery Method to study the Bible or some other book may wrestle with how the discussion and exploration are related to the seeker's offering and the responses during the prayer time. At times there is a direct connection between the two. With a Bible or book study, this is less likely to happen as the topic has been selected ahead of time. The topic for the discussion and exploration will most likely be different from the topic of the Prayer Model, and the two may seem disconnected from each other. Primarily, the relationship between the prayer and discussion lies in the way the prayer affects the quality of the discussion. The discipline of the Prayer Model helps participants to be more attentive and respectful listeners during the discussion and exploration. They tend to be more thoughtful in their analysis of the reading. Thus, the significant connection between the prayer and the discussion is more in the quality of the discussion than in its content. The prayer sets the tone for the discussion.

GROUP SPIRITUAL DIRECTION

Denise had been seeing a spiritual director for personal one-on-one spiritual counseling for several years. When her spiritual director moved away, Denise explored working with anther spiritual director, but none of the ones she contacted seemed to be a good match. She had also been participating in an adult education group that used the Spiritual Discovery Method, where she learned that the method could be used for group spiritual direction. In such a group, seekers would come together to accompany each other in their spiritual journeys. Denise decided to try group spiritual direction by gathering a group and using the Spiritual Discovery Method for their meeting structure.

Denise's group started with six people and soon grew to ten, which they felt was a comfortable size. At each monthly meeting, a seeker would bring a personal spiritual issue. During the following discussion and exploration, they discussed various topics related to the spiritual journey. Sometimes the topic was the same as the one raised by the seeker's presentation, as permitted by the seeker. At other times, the topic was sparked by the reading the group members had done or an experience someone had had since the last group meeting. Some of the topics were how the Spirit works in the world, development of spiritual disciplines, and the nature of God.

Over the years, some members moved away or left the group for other reasons, and newcomers joined the group. Members grew close and built strong relationships. In addition to their spiritual companionship, they walked with each other through a number of life's challenges and celebrations. One woman who moved away said, "I don't know how I will ever find another group like this one. I have grown so much and knew I always had someone to talk to here." Another said, "My relationship with God has deepened so much since I have joined this group." Denise found that the need she had felt after her spiritual director moved away was more than met by their group spiritual direction using the Spiritual Discovery Method.

PERSONAL DISCOVERY OPPORTUNITIES

Scott had been praying and reflecting about a call to ordained ministry. He assembled a group in his congregation to meet with him about his ministry discernment. They studied the Spiritual Discovery Method and used it throughout their sessions. In the process, group members developed especially meaningful relationships with each other as well as a deep appreciation for the Spiritual Discovery Method. They decided they wanted to continue meeting after they finished the discernment process with Scott. Since they no longer had a specific task and goal and weren't sure how to proceed, they gathered to reflect on their experience and discuss some possible next steps.

Throughout their time with Scott, group members had come to recognize how influential the Spiritual Discovery Method had been for the development of their own spiritual lives. One person described an "aha" moment of personal discovery when she had served as a compassionate observer in the Prayer Model. She realized that God was being a compassionate observer for her, and it changed the way she thought about God's love. Another said he had come to a new appreciation for communal prayer. The accountability to the group had helped another become more faithful to her personal prayer discipline. Others said that they had learned much about listening, how to appreciate silence, and discernment. As they reflected, it gradually became evident that focusing on their own spiritual development was a sufficient reason to continue meeting.

The group began to brainstorm about how the Spiritual Discovery Method could be used to structure their future meetings and guide them in their spiritual growth. The discernment skills they had learned while they worked with Scott were especially useful. These skills had often aided them in their own personal decision-making. The structure of the meetings would remain the same. Their focus, however, would be on developing their discernment skills, and they compiled a list of readings on that topic.

For the next several months the group met, and at each meeting, they did the Prayer Model, took a short break, and then discussed their reading on discernment skills. They noted the ways they used their growing skills in their own lives. One participant had been trying to decide whether to take a promotion that would require extensive time away from his family. He described how he was able to pray about his decision and discuss it thoroughly with his family. Another was trying to determine whether she should encourage her aging mother to move closer to her home so they could spend more time together. She found she had been open to considering a wider range of options as she pondered the decision. Others were pleased with how their practice in discernment helped with a number of smaller, everyday decisions. The Spiritual Discovery Method had helped group members become skilled in discernment.

During a discussion after some months of meeting, one of the group members imagined out loud what it would be like if they could share their discernment skills with other people in the congregation. Just as they had gathered with Scott while he considered ordained ministry, they could offer to pray and talk with others who were facing discernment challenges in their own lives. Group members could easily think of a number of folks who were considering career or personal life changes. They wondered if these folks might wish to bring their dilemmas to a discernment group such as theirs. They decided to offer the services of their group to members of the congregation, encouraging them to meet with them as guest seekers. They presented their plan to the congregational leadership and received its endorsement.

The group publicized their invitation, offering the opportunity for others to visit and take the place of the seeker. A visiting seeker would meet with a group member ahead of time to be introduced to the method. The seeker would then meet with the group, present her dilemma during the Prayer Model, and take part in a discussion in which they would together explore the seeker's dilemma. A visiting seeker could meet with the group for one or more sessions to discern about any type of decision.

They knew they needed to be attentive to how they welcomed their visitors and familiarized them with the Spiritual Discovery Method. Letting them know that the Prayer Model included periods of silence was important, as was the fact that what seekers presented was completely confidential.

Providing instructions on the role of the seeker and how to prepare was also significant. The seeker needed to know he could choose the topic of the discussion and exploration time. A description of the meeting structure and a list of group members would be helpful, as would assurance that the time-keeper would provide instructions through the Prayer Model. Orienting the visiting seeker and providing clear instructions and information was an important demonstration of care and hospitality.

Few people in the congregation came to the group with their discernment needs. Those who did so found it beneficial. One visiting seeker said that she had gained new insights into her decision and felt much more certain about it. Another described how he had felt immobilized by his situation, and the group had helped him see possibilities he had not considered before. A congregational leader was able to take what she discerned back to the leadership council. Her insight shed new light on a key decision.

Though their invitation to guest seekers had attracted only a few congregation members, the group was satisfied that the limited response was not a failure. They were focused on their own spiritual discernment as they met month to month, while at the same time remaining available to others who wished to visit as seekers. Their use of the Spiritual Discovery Method was an excellent way to meet the needs of group members who wanted to pray and discern together, while at the same time supporting the discernment needs of congregation members.

This type of group meets regularly whether or not there is a visitor as seeker. They practice the Spiritual Discovery Method with members bringing their own spiritual questions and dilemmas. Their discussion may be dedicated to exploring spiritual questions that arise or may be guided by a book or other reading. They may explore Biblical stories or study topics such as discernment, leadership, or personality type. Groups such as these that endure over time tend to be those that regard themselves first as a spiritual formation group for the members and secondly as a group that provides discernment support for the congregation.

CONFLICT MANAGEMENT

Chapel in the Pines was a small and aging congregation in the mountains of Colorado. They had recently become embroiled in a conflict about the style of music they used in their worship service. Concerned about their dwindling numbers, several people in the congregation thought they could attract new and younger members to their worship services if they added some contemporary music. Others insisted on singing only traditional hymns. Among the current members were a talented guitarist, a keyboard player, and a drummer. They were asked to lead the contemporary music that was added. For a while, members agreed to try a blended service using both contemporary music and traditional hymns.

It wasn't long, however, before some members started to complain about the new music. The congregational leadership, always concerned about losing people, desperately tried to address the situation, but without much success. Danny, a member of the leadership group, had served on a discernment group in his prior congregation. He wondered if the Spiritual Discovery Method might be useful in the current conflict.

Since I (Catherine) had taught Danny's original group the Spiritual Discovery Method, he contacted me and described the conflict in the congregation. We discussed how the method might be useful in managing the conflict. Danny went back to the leadership group and suggested the Spiritual Discovery Method to help deal with the conflict. Since efforts to resolve the conflict had been ineffective, the council was willing to try it. They invited me to come and facilitate a process of conflict management that would incorporate the Spiritual Discovery Method.

At our first meeting, we began by reviewing the Prayer Model with its roles and processes. Earlier, I had requested that the volunteer seeker summarize the conflict and share any thoughts and feelings she wished. Group members volunteered to serve as seeker, responders, and compassionate observers. We went into the prayer room and took our places in the circles.

The seeker began by describing how the conflict started and some key factors that caused the conflict to escalate. There had been some miscommunication as well as differences of opinion. Early efforts to resolve the conflict had only seemed to exacerbate the problem. Some members of the congregation had been critical of those with whom they disagreed. She admitted that she found it difficult to not get angry and to think objectively about the direction the congregation should take. She worried about how the conflict was affecting the congregation. It had been painful to see people taking sides. When she finished, we entered into the time of silence.

Out of the prayerful silence, the responders offered their gifts. One observed how animated the seeker had been during her presentation and how, even though they were on opposite sides of the issue, her description had helped him see her point of view and why she felt so strongly about it.

Another recalled a passage of scripture that encouraged faith communities to reconcile their differences. The last responder told the seeker how much she appreciated what the seeker had said and how important it was to hear all sides of the issue. We entered into silence.

When the seeker took her turn to speak again, she talked about how relieved she was to share her thoughts and what a blessing it was to be heard. She said that she felt more hopeful and that she was going to try to be more prayerful as the conflict continued to unfold in the congregation. She thanked the responders.

We moved our chairs into a single circle and began to debrief. We asked the seeker to share her thoughts on the process. She said that she felt safe sharing her strong feelings. She was overwhelmed by how deeply others had listened to her. She said that without the setting of the Prayer Model, she was not sure how she could have shared her feelings with the group at all. She told how she felt the care of the group, even those whom she knew disagreed with her, and that she felt closer to the others in the group because of the prayer experience.

During the discussion that followed, one participant said that even though there was disagreement in the group, she felt more open toward other group members. One member said he was able to listen to the seeker more intently and heard things that he had not heard before. He said that he began to understand that he needed to listen to others as well as the Spirit in the midst of this conflict. Another appreciated the intervals of silence during the prayer and how they helped him to listen and refocus on the presence of God. They discussed how they, as leaders, might take the same listening hearts that they had experienced in the Prayer Model out to other members of the congrega- tion. They wondered if they modeled good listening skills that it might en- courage good listening throughout the congregation. If the leadership was able to calmly hear what members of the congregation were saying, perhaps the level of tension would go down as people felt they were being heard. If congregational leaders were listening to the Spirit, perhaps other members would begin to listen to the Spirit as well. They explored more aspects of good listening and resolved to be good listeners through the next month before they met again.

At the next meeting, the congregational leaders said they were pleased with their listening experiment. Although there was still plenty of energy around the music conflict, it did seem that quiet listening had lowered the temperature a bit. Several members of the congregation told the leaders that they appreciated being heard and felt like they could trust the leaders to hear all sides of the issue. One person said she felt valued because the leaders had heard what she had to say when no one else would listen. Another said that he was impressed by how calm the leadership seemed to be.

Something had shifted in their life together—this was evident to everyone. The changes would be important as the group managed the conflict and the congregation moved ahead. Most people in the group agreed that they had experienced a deeper level of trust and had a new understanding of how important it was to listen carefully to the Spirit and to each other. In the months ahead, the quality of their regular meetings changed as the group grew in trust and it became less threatening to discuss divisive questions. They were encouraged that they could reach a workable resolution.

SUPPORT GROUP

Grace Church sponsored a support group for young mothers, providing child care and Bible study and, from time to time, a speaker on child rearing or self-care for moms. The group met each week for a couple of hours, and the young moms came to depend on and appreciate the time set aside for sharing with each other the joys and concerns about parenting. During one of their sessions, several of the moms talked about how little time or energy they had to attend in a more intentional way to their own spiritual needs. They felt that if they could find a way to do that they could also be better parents.

One mom had an idea which she shared with the others. She had been part of a group some months earlier that had used the Spiritual Discovery Method. Describing briefly how it worked and the benefit she had gained from the experience, she wondered if the moms' group might like to try it. They could learn and practice the Prayer Model and then use the discussion and exploration time to spiritually support each other, especially in parenting. Their discussion and exploration could be guided by a personal parenting concern brought by one of the members. Or they could read about parenting or view a short video which would provide a topic for their discussion and exploration time. They agreed that they would like to try the Spiritual Discovery Method at their next meeting.

As they gathered, one of the moms who had volunteered to serve as seeker told the group that she was struggling with how to handle her daughter's temper tantrums. She said she was particularly frustrated when her daughter misbehaved in public and that she was feeling herself running out of patience. That lack of patience was worrying her a lot. The responders shared their offerings of insight and inspiration, and the compassionate observers held the others in respectful silence and prayer.

When the group shifted out of the Prayer Model and debriefed their experience, the seeker told the others that it had felt good to be able to talk about her concerns and parenting questions. She had been relieved to admit to her frustration. She said she felt as though she was no longer alone in her dilemma. Others in the group said they felt honored to be trusted with such important sharing. One responder said that she had had similar experiences, which had made it a challenge to respond at all. The others said they had felt the same way—the seeker's story was familiar and difficult for many of the moms. The compassionate observers talked about how privileged it had made them feel to hold the seeker's sharing and responders' offerings in silence and prayer.

When the group regathered following a coffee break, the mom who had been a seeker said she'd be willing to offer her dilemma for the group discussion and exploration. Others in the group admitted they faced similar challenges and would be grateful to spend more time on the topic. The group members went on to discuss how they might respond to their child's temper tantrums. They commiserated with each other about the public embarrassment that was sometimes part of the parenting experience and strategized about how they could respond to their children in a healthy way and try some new parenting techniques. The moms talked about how they might support each other if it seemed that patience was running out. They agreed to report back to the group on how their new parenting techniques were working

Over the year, the moms covered many joys and difficulties of parenting. They said they felt encouraged and supported as they faced common challenges with their children. The group experience helped them to be better parents because they had learned new parenting techniques and knew they could call on their companions if they felt the need. Because they had practiced listening in the Prayer Model, many moms felt they could be better listeners with their children. Because they came together in prayer and discussion, they more faithfully attended to their own spiritual needs in the midst of everyday parenting.

SPIRITUAL RETREATS

Joyce was teaching a group of folks about the Enneagram, a personality inventory that has been used for centuries and whose purpose is developing personal spiritual self-understanding. They had been studying and discussing the Enneagram for about a year, exploring their own personality types and their relationships to spiritual growth. Joyce decided that she wanted to help her group members go even deeper into the spiritual aspects of the Enneagram so they could be more open to its invitations for spiritual growth. She planned a three day retreat. Because she was familiar with the Spiritual Discovery Method, Joyce realized it would be helpful as a framework for the retreat, so she arranged to use it throughout.

Joyce prepared for the retreat by recruiting four participants to serve as small group leaders. She asked them to read about the Spiritual Discovery Method and meet with her before the retreat so they could learn the method and experience it for themselves. The group leaders were instructed in how to lead their small groups through the Prayer Model, conduct the debriefing, and guide the discussion and exploration time.

Retreat participants arrived on the first evening for the opening session. Introductions were made and logistics were covered. For the duration of the retreat, they were divided into four groups of ten to twelve members each. They had instruction and did the Prayer Model for the first time. This was followed by a discussion and exploration of the practical uses of the Enneagram for spiritual growth. Over the next three days, the groups used the method to guide their prayer and discussion of various aspects of the Enneagram. They explored how the personality type indicator could guide participants as they examined their gifts and challenges. The Prayer Model provided each participant an opportunity to go deeper into his or her personal discovery, while the discussion offered a setting for more exploration of the wisdom of the Enneagram.

Joyce found that the Spiritual Discovery Method created the opportunity for participants to slow down and to reflect on the Enneagram and how it informed their spiritual experience. The silence helped participants listen to each other and encouraged a greater awareness of how the Spirit was speaking. Compassionate observation helped participants to be less judgmental of themselves and more open to what the Enneagram had to offer. The discussion and exploration, which was shaped by the prayer, facilitated learning from each other with greater openness. Joyce thought the Spiritual Discovery

Method was a positive addition to the retreat because it helped participants take time to reflect and pray about how they might address some difficult personality traits and relational habits. Since the method had so successfully supported the participants in their self-examination and spiritual growth, Joyce decided that she would use the format for future retreats.

RETIREMENT TRANSITION GROUP

Michael's busy practice as a life coach included several people who were beginning a transition into retirement. He thought it might be helpful for these clients to meet and have an opportunity to support each other as they anticipated the changes that would come with retirement. An idea for a design for meetings of such a group came from his own personal experience with the Spiritual Discovery Method.

A retirement transition group such as Michael contemplated would be made up of a variety of people, not all of them active in a religious tradition. Michael believed that the elements of quiet reflection and listening inherent in the Spiritual Discovery Method would enrich the experience for all participants in the retirement transition group. So he decided to adapt the Spiritual Discovery Method for a non-religious setting by renaming it the Listening/ Reflection Method and modifying some of its language.

Michael drafted a description of the Listening/Reflection Method. The overall design of the Spiritual Discovery Method remained unchanged and included check-in, the listening/reflection time, debriefing, a break, exploration and discussion, and a closure event. The process of the listening/reflection time was described using terms such as "silent reflection" for "prayer" and "circle of confidentiality" for "sacred space." While retaining the description of the seeker and responder, he represented the role of compassionate observer as one of offering companionship, respectful listening, and silent reflection rather than one of prayer. A final alteration Michael made was replacing the prayer chime with instructions for the leader to guide the group through the process with verbal instructions at the appropriate times.

Michael recruited folks to join his retirement transition group. He described the purpose of the group and briefly how it would function. They would meet once a month. Each time one member would volunteer to serve as seeker, sharing a retirement-related dilemma or challenge in his or her own experience. The group would also discuss a topic related to retirement transition. Silence, listening, and reflection would be significant components of their meetings. Several people agreed to give it a try, and the date for their first meeting was set.

When the group gathered for its first meeting, Michael began by summarizing the points he had made in his recruitment conversations. He then asked them to introduce themselves, briefly describing their anticipated retirement and sharing their hopes for the group sessions to come. Michael offered a detailed outline of the structure of their future meetings, handing out the description of the method he had prepared. He talked about the norms for the group meetings, most importantly the confidentiality required of all participants. He asked for questions and invited discussion about the Listening/Reflection Method and the group meetings as a whole. Michael concluded the meeting by requesting a volunteer seeker for the next meeting and proposing a topic for discussion at that meeting: "Freedoms of Retirement."

The group met regularly for nine months and at their planned closure event offered a number of final reflections on their own journeys and how the Listening/Reflection Method had worked for them. One said it had been very useful to have a place where he could describe the challenges he was discovering as he approached retirement. Several agreed with him and added that it was equally helpful to know that others were facing similar challenges. Another said she had found the seekers' presentations very enlightening because they introduced topics she hadn't considered and she recognized that they were her issues also.

A number of the group members admitted that the method had helped them become better listeners. One man said he particularly appreciated the quiet, contemplative component of the gatherings because it reminded him of how busy his present life was and how little it allowed for him to be silent and reflective. He said he was looking forward to enjoying more such leisure in his future retirement but also recognized the importance of practicing this discipline so he could more fully enjoy such moments. Group members said they generally felt better prepared for the changes and challenges that would come with their retirements.

As they ended their time together, a couple of members said they could imagine using the Listening/Reflection Method in other groups. Michael concluded that this adaptation of the Spiritual Discovery Method had been successful and found himself pondering the use of it for other groups, perhaps groups anticipating other sorts of life transitions.

SECULAR TASK FORCE

Roger owned a company that provided technical support and consultation for small businesses. He had successfully grown the company from a one man operation to one of fifty employees. With the recession, however, the company was facing difficulties, including a decline in customer satisfaction. Roger decided to form a task force to evaluate efficiency and customer service and make recommendations for improvement. He asked each of his six managers to appoint two people to the group and charged the group to conduct an evaluation and present its recommendations within eight weeks. The group was to begin its work with a three day retreat and then take one day out of each work week to focus on its new responsibility. They were free to determine how they would go about accomplishing their work.

One member of the group was familiar with the Spiritual Discovery Method. She introduced it to the group at the retreat, replacing its spiritual language with secular language. She made a case for using the method by explaining that it would help them listen carefully to each other and reflect deeply about what they heard. Several expressed enthusiasm for engaging in a process that was so different from what they usually experienced in their work environment. Some thought the method might free up creative thinking and lead to deeper insights. They decided to try it.

Group members agreed that the topics they would bring to the listening and reflection time would be shaped by their personal experiences as employees of the company. These would include both challenges and celebrations, which would heighten their awareness of what was working as well as what was not. They also devised a plan for interviewing employees and customers, examining business records, and gathering data. All this information would guide the discussion and exploration time. What the seeker brought to the listening and reflection time was more personal, while the discussion and exploration time was shaped by the data they collected.

As the weeks passed, the use of the method helped task force members practice listening. They were able to take their new skills into interviews with customers and employees. They carefully examined and reflected on the data they gathered and the personal experiences the group members had brought into the group's listening and reflection times. In the final three weeks of the group's work, individual members shared their creative ideas for organizational change during the listening and reflection time. The discussion time was devoted to refining the ideas and developing the action plans. By the time the task force made its final recommendations to Roger, the data had been carefully examined, personal experiences of employees and customers had been considered, and creative solutions to the company's challenges had been proposed.

Members of the task force described their time together as the best workplace process in their professional experience. They thought they had listened carefully to each other and to all who had participated in the interviews. Their discussions had been creative and productive, with a tone of cooperation and teamwork. They were pleased with the suggestions they proposed because they were thorough and constructive. Roger was very grateful for the work and recommendations of the task force.

In our examination of various groups and how they use the Spiritual Discovery Method, we have seen how it can be adapted to serve a number of situations. It can be used by ongoing groups as well as groups that meet to complete a specific task. It may be used for short or long term objectives, for decision-making, conflict resolution, relationship building, or personal learning and growth. Groups that use the Spiritual Discovery Method may be comprised of people from various religious backgrounds and faith traditions, or no faith tradition at all. Group members need only be interested in wrestling with questions and willing to participate in a reflective practice. The use of the method is limited only by the imaginations of its practitioners.

Conclusion

Throughout this book, we have described the Spiritual Discovery Method as a means of making decisions in community. We have shown how the method facilitates thoughtful discernment, encouraging groups and individuals to attend to *how* they make decisions. We have described different ways the Spiritual Discovery Method can be used for the benefit of groups and individuals. We have examined the structure of the Spiritual Discovery Method, looking at the Vennard Prayer Model, each of its roles, reflecting on the role of compassionate observer in particular. The mechanics of conducting the method have been identified. Essentials and challenges have been discussed.

We have also examined the skills that practitioners develop as they use the Spiritual Discovery Method. After practicing the method, participants become better listeners. Seekers are more thoughtful and trust their inner wisdom when they search for responses to struggles they encounter. Responders become attentive to the Spirit and comfortable with offering what comes to them. Compassionate observers, over time, are more able to remain still and silent, aware of what is happening around them. They have found that they are less judgmental of themselves and others. They are more open to new possibilities.

We have seen how these skills can be put to use in the world, ready to be called upon at the service of decision-making. When a quick decision is required, the skills are there. The decision-maker has listened to herself, to others, and to the Spirit. She has prayed, and remained self-aware and open. She has let go of judgment and observed with compassion. The "muscle memory" has become practiced and dependable. The skills practiced in the method have proven to be transformational in the lives of participants and their communities.

The skills are, however, only some of the gifts that the Spiritual Discovery Method offers. The method also engages the gift of holy imagination which encourages the seeker to perceive and create possibilities and then to choose among them. Holy imagination is often hopeful in that it reveals new potential and envisions what can be. It can be a source of courage that enables venturing into an unknown future.

Use of the Spiritual Discovery Method invites awareness of holy presence. It creates the opportunity for participants to make room for the Spirit and wait expectantly for the Spirit to speak. They take the time to observe and listen. Participants become skillful at making decisions in the presence of the Spirit, seeing with the eyes of God and hearing as God hears. The process leads to a decision, to discovery, to a new creation. God's love becomes a creative force in the process and decision-making becomes an art.

Through the practice of the Spiritual Discovery Method, the participant changes and grows. The method becomes a powerful instrument for change and spiritual growth. It is wise for readers to use the method with the expectation that continued practice will lead to growth and change for individuals and for the groups and communities that use it. Its faithful practice will lead to greater self examination, self awareness, and growth. The method has the potential of being a significant instrument of spiritual transformation. The participant becomes a new creation.

The Spirit is present and moving in the process of coming to a decision. The decision leads to action and change is inevitable. Life will be different. As you practice the Spiritual Discovery Method and listen to the voice of the Spirit speaking to you, our hope is that you will be celebrating the new creation you become. With the information set forth in this book, you have all you need to move ahead. Now you are invited to begin your new venture into decision-making and discovery.

Notes

6. A MODIFIED PRAYER MODEL

1. Palmer J. Parker, *A Hidden Wholeness: The Journey toward an Undivided Life* (San Francisco: Jossey-Bass, 2004), 132.
2. Ibid, 134.

8. DISCERNMENT

1. Joann Wolski Conn, ed., *Women's Spirituality: Resources for Christian Development* (Mahwah, NJ: Paulist Press, 1986), 3.
2. Danny E. Morris and Charles M. Olsen, *Discerning God's Will Together: A Spiritual Practice for the Church* (Bethesda, MD: Alban Books, 1997), 13.

11. ESSENTIALS FOR THE SPIRITUAL DISCOVERY METHOD

1. Frederick Buechner, *Telling the Truth: The Gospel as Tragedy, Comedy, and Fairy Tale* (New York: HarperCollins, 1977), 8.

13. THE POWER OF COMPASSION AND OBSERVATION

1. Jane E. Vennard, *Fully Awake and Truly Alive: Spiritual Practices to Nurture Your Soul* (Woodstock, VT: Skylight Paths, 2013), 135.
2. Thomas R. Kelly, *A Testament of Devotion* (San Francisco: HarperSanFrancisco, 1996), 4.

3. Ibid, 80.
4. Ibid, 81.